Principles of Asymmetrical Warfare

Principles of Asymmetrical Warfare

How to Beat Islamo-fascists at Their Own Game

Robert T. Uda, MBA, MS, BS²

iUniverse, Inc.
New York Lincoln Shanghai

Principles of Asymmetrical Warfare
How to Beat Islamo-fascists at Their Own Game

Copyright © 2007 by Robert T. Uda

iUniverse books may be ordered through booksellers or by contacting:

iUniverse
2021 Pine Lake Road, Suite 100
Lincoln, NE 68512
www.iuniverse.com
1-800-Authors (1-800-288-4677)

ISBN-13: 978-0-595-42818-2 (pbk)
ISBN-13: 978-0-595-68189-1 (cloth)
ISBN-13: 978-0-595-87156-8 (ebk)
ISBN-10: 0-595-42818-5 (pbk)
ISBN-10: 0-595-68189-1 (cloth)
ISBN-10: 0-595-87156-9 (ebk)

Printed in the United States of America

Dedication

Principles of Asymmetrical Warfare: How to Beat Islamo-fascists at Their Own Game is dedicated to Dr. Michael Savage and the Pendleton 8 and their families. Because of political correctness (PC), the Pendleton 8 was unfairly and unjustly treated by the United States Government and the United States Marine Corps (USMC). They were considered guilty until proven innocent instead of vice versa.

Eighty percent of the royalties received from the sale of this book will be donated to the eight Pendleton 8 families. The family members are innocent victims, yet they suffered too from the tragedies of war. War is hell! The US Government and its faulty legal system have mistreated these Pendleton 8 heroes. If any of them are incarcerated for their trumped-up charges, President George W. Bush should pardon them at the twilight of his presidency.

Contents

Preface

Principles of Asymmetrical Warfare: How to Beat Islamo-fascists at Their Own Game provides the principles, strategies, and tactics available to the Bush Administration in winning and ending the War in Afghanistan, War in Iraq, and the overall War on Terrorism. Some of the strategies and tactics may appear extreme to a civilized country as the United States of America. However, we should know about and understand these strategies and tactics in the event that we must use them because we are about to be totally annihilated, conquered, and/or placed in bondage.

I have quoted much of the ideas from Sun Tzu, General George S. Patton, Jr., and Dr. Michael Savage (the greatest talk show host alive). Our Administration has made a major mistake by not learning from great warriors like Sun Tzu and General George Patton. Our Administration makes an even bigger mistake by ignoring the thoughts and ideas of Dr. Savage, a man of great intellect. All other ideas not quoted from someone else are mine only. Many of the ideas are just common sense, which seem to be lacking in our politicians, Administration, and military generals. They just do not know how to fight and win an asymmetrical war. This book provides them with fresh ideas on fighting the Islamo-fascists and winning the War on Terrorism.

If you disagree with anything that I have written in this book, I encourage you to write me and voice your disagreement. I always like to hear and learn about other people's views on whatever I write. Never do I believe that I know all truth on anything. I am always willing to change my views if someone comes up with contrary responses that make sense to me. That being said, I look forward to hearing from you.

All writings and opinions in this book are solely mine. Any error would be my error only. If you find errors, please bring them to my attention. We will correct them in subsequent editions of this book. I hope you enjoy the real-life stories in this book as I thoroughly have enjoyed living and writing about them. Thank you.

Robert T. Uda
San Marcos, California
March 2007

Chapter 1

What if Japan Attacked the US Today?

BREAKING NEWS! Japan attacks Pearl Harbor again, but this time they win! This is a serious (i.e., not funny) satirical fairy tale of America under today's political milieu.

If the Japanese attacked the United States today as they did on December 7, 1941, this fairy tale indicates a different outcome just because of today's political climate in the United States and the world. This is a completely new ballgame—a different scenario.

Dateline Breaking News: **Friday, December 7, 2007**

Most Horrific Event since 9/11/01

Kamikaze Attack. Japanese *kamikaze* bombers fly airplanes into American warships moored at Pearl Harbor, Hawaii, killing nearly 3,000 people early on a clear, peaceful Friday (not Sunday this time) morning. Additional, a full-scale invasion of San Francisco and "Sin City" Las Vegas is in full swing with *kamikaze* bombers hitting with impunity major high-rise buildings (such as the Transamerica Building) in central Frisco.

20-million Americans Die in Nuclear Holocaust. Nuclear weapons, transported by Japan Airlines (JAL) and All Nippon Airlines (ANA), commercial passenger carriers, and Nippon Cargo Airlines (NCA), commercial cargo carriers, hit other major cities throughout the United States. *It is payback time!* They are trading kilotons on Hiroshima and Nagasaki for megatons on the cities of New York, Los Angeles, Chicago, Houston, and Philadelphia ... an instantaneous vaporization of only about 20

It is payback time!

million people. The nation is in shock! Why? Why are people in shock? We have been slowly sliding down a slippery slope for the past 50 years to end in the only way we could go, which is down the tubes.

Nuclear Power for Electrical Generation. Because Japan needed to protect itself after World War II ended and also to develop nuclear power for generating electricity (so says Emperor Hideki Tojo), Russia and China encouraged and helped Japan with nuclear technology to develop nuke weapons. Hence, Japan started manufacturing thousands of nuclear bombs and warheads, and we allowed them to do it. Furthermore, Japan paid the Sino-Soviets lots of money. As Michael Reagan likes to repeat that old saying, "Follow the money trail." *Apparently, money is the catalyst for all progress in this world.*

> *Apparently, money is the catalyst for all progress in this world.*

It's All the President's Fault. All Americans are glued to their television sets, and they flood the telephone lines calling 911 (How ironic!), military bases, elected officials, family, and friends. The mainstream media says that it is all President George W. Bush's fault. The mainstream media tends to publish op-ed page material as news on the front page of their respective rags. It is a shame that *The National Enquirer* publishes more accurate and honest news then does the mainstream media.

Politicians Run the War. Our military cannot wage an effective war to win because the politicians are running the war. They care too much about following the Geneva Convention to the tee. The Democrats strive for power by fighting the Republican Administration tooth-and-nail on every initiative taken. Roadside bombs and mines, placed along all major highways and freeways throughout the United States by Japanese terror cells, kill thousands of motorists running helter-skelter to-and-fro trying to determine what to do.

Awakening a Sleeping Pigmy. After the attack on Pearl Harbor, Japan's combined naval fleet commander, Admiral Isoroku Yamamoto, said " ... *it seems all we have done is awakened a sleeping giant.*" Today, the enemy would consider the "giant" as a "pigmy." This is the message of secular progressives (SPs) of America (Bill O'Reilly's term) are sending to all terrorists and anti-American nations throughout the world, i.e.,

> *The United States is no more a giant but, instead, is a pigmy.*

the United States is no more a giant but, instead, is a pigmy. Yes, the enemy is using the SPs to achieve their ends. After Japan wins the war, the SPs who think they will receive a pass by the enemy will instead get their heads summarily sawed off in mass-beheading events. Our enemies will first use and later abuse SPs to achieve their ends.

A Conspiracy

"He knew about it," shrieked ex-presidential candidate and loser Al Gore, "George Bush lied to us!" "It's a vast right-wing conspiracy," chanted the Democrat presidential hopeful Senator Hillary Rodham Clinton. Screaming at the top of his lungs, Howard Dean said, "The way to beat the president is to stand up to him and be proud of it, by giving people a reason to vote again." All of these extremist, left wing, radical Democrats were successful in wresting control of both houses of Congress in the recent midterm elections. Sad days are ahead of us because of the sheer stupidity of the Republicans.

Deafening Silence from Japanese Americans

Mum is the Word. Not very unlike the growing Arab/Muslim/Islamite (AMI) population in the United States, Americans of Japanese Ancestry (AJAs) are noticeably mum, for "mum is the word." Yes, they "see not-ting, hear not-ting, and say not-ting." What a bunch of monkeys! They do not condemn this dastardly deed by their mother country! Their deafening silence makes one wonder on which side of the line they stand. "You are either with us or against us," stated President Bush. Why, we hear absolutely no word out of Gardena, California, a haven of AJA folks eating their sushi and tempura along with sticky rice and soy sauce. Not a single word … *nada*, notting, *non*, zilch, *nyet*, *nein*, zero!

Patriots or Fellow Travelers? Why will not the AJA population speak up for America? Are they afraid of being lynched or assassinated by Japanese terrorist cells within the United States? Are they "fellow travelers" who go along with the idea of world domination as expounded by the extremist, radical, communistic Shinto and Buddhist fundamentalists who believe in *hara-kiri* (suicide by disembowelment) or as they say in America, *hari-kari*? Or are they like the SPs who will "wait and see" as to who will be the winner and then join the winning team just a few moments prior to getting their heads lopped off (or decapitated) with a dull *Samurai* sword by terrorist leader Abu "Musubi" al-Zarqawi san?

Congress Declares War ... NOT!

The Disloyal Opposition. The President cannot garner a majority vote for a formal Declaration of War against the Empire of Japan because the entire SP Democrat establishment, including the Democrat Black Caucus and Congressperson Maxine Waters, is dead against going to war with such a peace-loving country as Japan. *Fifty-one percent of the members of Congress vote against declaring war on Japan!* Of course, Jesse Jackson, Al Sharpton, and Charlie Rangel make the circuit of the mainstream media. They tell everyone that it would be racist to declare war on a little 'ole minority country like the looks of Japan, which is only the size of the State of California for goodness sake!

> *Fifty-one percent of the members of Congress vote against declaring war on Japan.*

Traitor's Traitors. Political hacks like Teddy Kennedy, Howard Dean, John Kerry, Jack Murtha, and Hillary Clinton holler in Congress that it was the Bush Administration that caused the Japanese to attack the United States because we are too insennnsitive (as Michael Savage would say) to their feeeeelings. We should refraaain from hurting anyone's feeeeelings. Senate majority leader Harry Reid declares, "We have a Republican cover-up here!"

Catering to the Enemy. After all, we have mistreated the Japanese so badly ever since we put them back on their feet following their first attack on Pearl Harbor and subsequent defeat caused by our Democrat President Harry Truman who unfaaaairly and insensitiiiiiively dropped "Fat Boy" and "Little Boy" A-bombs on Hiroshima and Nagasaki, respectively. Never mind that he saved millions of lives (both Japanese and American lives) by abruptly terminating the war with two little "shock and awe" bangs!

Collateral Liquidation. *If we ever repeated that nuking of Japan today, there would be huge outcries from the left of "collateral damage."* On a second thought, they would probably create a new politically correct term called "collateral liquidation" ... not to mention "fratricide."

> *If we ever repeated that nuking of Japan today, there would be huge outcries from the left of "collateral damage."*

We Americans are bad dudes! That is why the world hates us so much … so says the liberal left.

A Conspiracy. Furthermore, according to the liberals, the Japanese attack on Pearl Harbor was a conspiracy concocted by George Bush and Carl Rove (a puppeteer) who they say, basically, is running the country along with Dick Chaney. The Democrats call George Bush an idiot, yet they are sure that he is at least smart enough to concoct, along with the Japanese, a carefully planned conspiratorial self-attack on Pearl Harbor (sort of like the conspirators who claimed that President Franklin D. Roosevelt got Japan to attack Pearl Harbor the first time around). Apparently, the Democrats are quite adept at simultaneously speaking out of both sides of their mouth. Native Americans call it "speaking with forked tongue" or, in other words, lying.

Entitlement Programs. Instead, the AJAs in Congress, headed by Senator Daniel Inouye from Hawaii, formed the "Yellow Caucus" and fought for "gimmees" AKA "give me's" and other such "handouts." *They don't want a hand; they just want a handout.* In other words, give me a fish; don't teach me how to fish because I don't want to work for my meals. They call it the politically correct term, "entitlement programs" … as if anyone was entitled to any entitlements. The Yellow Caucus would blame the Administration for all of its woes and constantly cry out that they were victims of racism, prejudice, and discrimination. Consequently, they screamed for reparations. Yes, we are a "you owe me" society.

> *They don't want a hand; they just want a handout.*

Tokyo Rose

Communist News Network. The world public views Tokyo Rose as akin to a hip-hop rock star. She makes daily Communist News Network (CNN) reports of Japan's successes on all fronts of their declared war by Emperor Hideki Tojo on the United States. In the latest Gallup, Zogby, and Roper polls, we find that 90 percent of the American public:

- Supports the Japanese winning the war

- Says that it was the US's fault that Japan had attacked us because we had provoked them

- Rationalizes that we are not in a real war but are experiencing criminal actions that local police departments can easily handle

Democrats Revel in Our Defeat. The power-hungry, SP Democrat Party headed by Howard Dean is thrilled with the defeats of American soldiers dying daily on all fronts. They feel that more filled body bags the better to support their position on the war. The press is very good at keeping a super-accurate daily body count and showing visual plots that illustrate a meteoric exponential rise in the body-count curve. Neat, huh? That is freedom of the press for you.

Freedom of Religion ... Except for Christians

Freedom of Religion. Like the Islamic *Imams*, Japanese Shinto leaders preach in their Shinto shrines throughout the country "Death to America" and other such friendly epithets. Loser Al Gore accepts campaign money from these shrines, so they obviously cannot all be that bad. The SPs in American think it is "cute" and that the Japanese Shinto leaders have their "rights" to preach whatever they want to because we have Freedom of Religion in this country. Hence, all of the Shinto and Buddhist temples in Hawaii, California, and other Japanese-American strongholds in the US are allowed to house Japanese insurgents from Japan. After all, Michael Savage, the genius, would say, "We don't want to huuuurt their feeeelings!"

Christians are Bad for America. Additionally, since the US Constitution's Bill of Rights says that we can own and bear arms, it is okay for the shrines to store caches of weaponry, bombs, and ammunition. After all, it is for their own self-defense against racist, right wing, conservative, Christian Republicans. To the SPs, America has freedom of religion for all world religions with the exception of Christianity. They feel that Christians are bad for America. Just ask Rosie O'Donnell and others of the Hollywood elite or Hollywood Mafia.

> *To the SPs, America has freedom of religion for all world religions with the exception of Christianity.*

Internment Camps

Internment Camps are Good. During the first go-around in World War II, we incarcerated good AJAs in internment camps. *Wikipedia* defines *internment* as "the imprisonment or confinement of people, commonly in large groups, without due process of law and a trial. An internment camp or concentration camp is a large detention center created for political opponents, enemy aliens, specific ethnic or religious groups, civilians of a critical war-zone, or other groups of people, often during a war."[1]

Pacifists Aid and Abet the Enemy. What was good for the AJAs then should be good for the AJAs now. However, because of the weak-on-defense, "cut-and-run" Democrats and weak-kneed, pacifist SPs in America on this second go-around, AJAs are free to spy, plot, commit terrorist acts, picket, demonstrate, burn the American flag, and dance in the streets whenever the Japanese terrorists behead captured American soldiers, win a big battle, or achieve victory in the continental US. Regarding pacifists, President Teddy Roosevelt said, "*The pacifist is as surely a traitor to his country and to humanity as [is] the most brutal warmonger.*"[2] Rough Rider Teddy makes good sense.

The Government Fiddles While America Burns. Only in America (that is, only in today's America) can these things go on when we are in a War on Terror or, in this story's case, a war with Japan. How sweet it is! *Nero fiddles while Rome burns. Analogously, our US government fiddles while America burns.* Under these conditions, there is no way Japan could ever lose the war with America!

> *Nero fiddles while Rome burns. Analogously, our US government fiddles while America burns.*

The Mainstream Media

Failing to Report the Truth. Japanese Americans are peeeeacfully assembling (of course, it's their Bill of Rights too), rioting in the streets, and burning thousands of automobiles (as was done in France). Yet the mainstream media (ABC,

---

1. From *Wikipedia*, the free encyclopedia, extracted on 9/14/06 from http://en.wikipedia.org/wiki/Internment.

2. Extracted on 9/15/06 from Teddy Roosevelt Quotes found at URL http://www.teddyroosevelt.com/teddy_roosevelt_quotes.htm.

CBS, NBC, CNN, *New York Times*, *Los Angeles Times*, and Fox News, which seems to be moving in the same direction as all the others) fails to report any of these activities. In fact, you only hear about the truth on talk radio … mainly from the greatest talk-show host alive, i.e., Michael Savage.

Paints US Military as Bad and Evil. During WW II, the press, in cartoons and written caricatures, painted a picture of the Japanese and Nazis as beasts, monsters, and wretched killers. Today, it is another story. The press paints President George Bush as the antagonist and the enemy as the protagonist. The mainstream media depicts the United States as the party in the wrong and the US military as bad and evil. Sad.

Worst Terrorist in the World. A future Catholic priest wrote in a blog that George Bush was the "worst terrorist in world history."[3] A supposedly more noted figure, singer Harry Belafonte, was speaking as a private citizen, not a UNICEF (United Nations International Children's Emergency Fund; now United Nations Children's Fund) goodwill ambassador, when he called President Bush 'the greatest terrorist in the world,' said the United Nations (UN) children's agency.[4] With friends like these, who needs enemies!

> *Down with America … down with the Great Satan!*

Political Correctness. The national press started showing nasty cartoons regarding the Shinto and Buddhist bibles. The Japanese people in Japan and other Far Eastern religions throughout the Pacific Rim were up in arms. They organized huge demonstrations, which broke out in riots and ranting *"Down with America … down with the Great Satan!"* The American Communist-Leaning Union (ACLU), Amnesty International, Human Rights Watch, and other such left-wing groups started beating on the press and Administration to become more "politically correct." So much for freedom of the press and free speech!

Hate America First. Thus, now, there are no nasty cartoons of our enemies shown in the national mainstream media. Instead, only nasty cartoons of George Bush, of our dying soldiers, of our military establishment, and of the United

---

3.   <future.catholic.priest@private.com> wrote in message news:1ntms0thirn97uitnrhlqicd0 hltnfv6ta@4ax.com. Extracted on 9/14/06 from URL http://www.groupsrv.com/religion/about94839.html.

4.   From *The Geeze*, which was updated on 14 JAN 2006—11:46 AM PST. Extracted on 9/14/06 from URL http://www.geeze.us/news-archives/jan-10-2006.htm.

States government drawn by the "hate-America-first" artists and cartoonists. After all, it is only done in jest. They're not hurting anyone. Our nation is going down the tubes, but nobody is getting hurt by those cartoons … yet.

Wiretapping and Intercepting Overseas Calls

The radical, liberal SP judges in America do not allow the President, his Administration, and the National Security Agency (NSA) to tap into any calls originating from Japan to their terrorist spy cells in America. They legislate from the bench and create their own twisted laws for all of us to follow. The Administration *cannot* tap the phones of members of Japanese terrorist cells in the United States. After all, the terrorists maintain their "right to privacy" even as they work to castrate America.

Shinto and Buddhist Temples are Safe Zones

No, we cannot enter, bomb, or destroy any of the Shinto and Buddhist temples and/or shrines. Additionally, Al Gore (the screamer), who receives campaign contributions from them for his next possible attempt at the presidency, supports their rights as a religious organization and as protected by the Constitution. *Politics makes strange bedfellows, right?* At any rate, these sacred temples and shrines are good because they harbor Japanese terror cells and hold large caches of guns, bombs, ammunition, and weapons of mass destruction (WMD). According to liberals, that's okay because Bush lied. There are no WMDs!

> *Politics makes strange bedfellows, right?*

Courts

Revolving Door. As quickly as we capture Japanese terrorists, the courts in the US just as quickly release them. A few weeks of incarceration is too much and too inhumane. "We don't want to hurt their feelings," said the Amnesty International representative. We want to be friennnnds with the enemy. Then, maybe, they won't hit us again. Right!

Blame America First Crowd. We do not want to violate their civil rights and civil liberties because the ACLU, a radical leftist organization, would be on our case. Hence, the ACLU, Amnesty International, and Human Rights Watch are fighting to protect the rights of all alien Japanese (both foreign and domestic) who are out to liquidate us. The SP courts, along with their similarly SP judges and these seditious groups, protect the enemy, support criminals, and ignore the plight of victims. *These people constitute the "Blame America First" crowd. They are despicable!*

> *These people constitute the "Blame America First" crowd. They are despicable!*

Terrorists to Torture Extremist SPs. Even though the terrorists are torturing our citizens, we do not torture them back because we are a ciiiiiivilized people. However, that is fine because they are just torturing the captured bellicose Hollywood elite, extreme left-win politicians, extremist SP educators, and whacko left-wing judges who are legislating from the bench.

Artistic Expression. Additionally, daily on television, the nice, civilized terrorists graphically behead with dull samurai swords and carpenter saws a few of the more choice candidates (and you know who they are). Furthermore, resourceful entrepreneurs record the beheadings on CDs and sell them in Blockbuster Video stores for the young children to buy and view. The SP Hollywood elite call it free, artistic expression (a Bohemian art form). Nice!

Illegal Aliens

A Big Mess. Illegal alien Japanese from Japan circuitously flock into the United States through the porous free-trade borders of Canada and Mexico. After all, we are now just one huge, happy, "Globalist" family with free borders, free trade, one currency, *mucho* languages, numerous compartmented cultures, and one real gargantuan mess. If people would only listen to Michael Savage's "borders, language, and culture" philosophy, we would be much better off as a nation.

> *We are just one blended mass or, should I say, mess?*

Seamless Society. Anymore, we have no borders, no national language, and no recognizable American culture. *We are just one blended mass or, should I say, mess?* People never listen to Michael Savage, a voice screaming from deep in the wilderness, pleading for "borders, language, and culture." Now, we distinguish nothing. *We are just one humongous seamless society … not a melting pot, but just one big, fat pot. Indeed, we are a "pot" society.*

Taking Advantage of the System. The alien Japanese start using our hospitals and doctors. They start attending our elementary schools, high schools, and colleges. They also figured out how to get on the welfare rolls. They never need to pay any taxes because they generally get paid "under the table." If they need a social security card to get a job, they steal one or get a fake card. What a great country we have here!

> *We are just one humongous seamless society … not a melting pot, but just one big, fat pot. Indeed, we are a "pot" society.*

A Nation of Outlaws. It's easy when you have the SPs helping you, mayors of our cities designating their cities as cities of refuge, sanctuaries, havens, or asylums for the poor, downtrodden, and needy illegal aliens who are, after all, human beings too. Some religious leaders say that breaking the law to help the poor is righteousness in action because we are satisfying a higher law. Bull! If we disagree with a particular law, disobey that law! *America was a nation founded on laws. Now, we are a nation of nothing but outlaws.* We have creeping socialism in action.

> *America was a nation founded on laws. Now, we are a nation of nothing but outlaws.*

Turning Japanese. The employers in the country welcome the Japanese workers because they are nice, smart, hard working, honest, and they keep to themselves (But watch out! They have a hidden agenda.). After all, we need those aliens to work our flower gardens, man our laundry and dry cleaning establishments, and cook our fast foods. After all, they are only doing the kind of work that average Americans would not do. Right! Now, the Japanese are demanding that we teach everyone in our schools, you guessed it, the Japanese language. There was an old 1980s hit tune that went like so:

I'm turning Japanese,
Turning Japanese,
Turning Japanese,

I really think so,
Think so.

Diversity is Perversity. Isn't it so sweet to have diversity and multiculturalism in America? Now, everyone is eating sushi, dried squid, sticky rice, and sashimi (raw fish). Good, no? Furthermore, everybody will be receiving forced plastic surgery on the eyes and will sport Asian eyes because "yellow is in."

Driver's License and the Vote. Oh, what really is interesting now is that the alien Japanese can now obtain driver's licenses. Prior to the passing of that SP law, they just drove anyway with neither a driver's license nor collision/liability insurance. To boot, they now can vote for the next SP whacko president of the United States. It is no wonder that this is the land of the free and the home of the brave. It is no wonder that this is the land of plenty.

Unlimited Rights. This is also the land of unlimited rights whether a citizen or alien. Everyone has unlimited rights here ... the liberals call it human rights and civil rights. If you are human, you have the right to live, work, and commit crimes in America. If you are a civilian, then you have a right to live, work, and commit heinous crimes in America. How great it is! It is no wonder this is the greatest country in the world. Wow! What a life! *It's time to wake up, America!*

> *It's time to wake up, America!*

Japan to Run Our Major Ports

Isn't it nice that President Bush wants Japan to run our ports in Honolulu, Los Angeles, San Francisco, Seattle, New York, and Mississippi? Hey, the Japanese can be trusted, for they are a trustworthy people. Japan, Inc., is making an overture to purchase the company that manages six of our major ports just as the United Arab Emirates (UAE) attempted to do until their was a huge backlash from grassroots America. This time, the sale will go through, and the Japanese midget submarines will maneuver and triumph. *It's payback time!*

> *It's payback time!*

Japan to Grow New, More Lucrative Crop

Learning good lessons from the Afghanis, Japan has stopped growing rice and, instead, started growing poppy. After all, poppy makes good heroin, and heroin brings in more money than does rice. Yes, as Michael Reagan says, "follow the money trail," and you find the source of every problem, mystery, and everything illegal.

> *"Follow the money trail."*
>
> **Michael Reagan**

Imperial Japan Conquers the USA

Surrender and One-world Government. So there you go. On the largest battleship of the Imperial Empire of Japan moored in New York Harbor, a broken President Bush signs the surrender documents with Emperor Hideki Tojo in charge of the ceremony. There is no General Douglas MacArthur or General George S. Patton, Jr., present. The United Nations Building becomes the World Headquarters for the one-world government of the Empire of Japan. Everyone in the world will henceforth communicate only in the Japanese language.

> *We have met the enemy, and he is us.*
>
> **Walt Kelly, *Pogo***

Bleeding-heart SPs. All SPs in the country are asking, "Why us?" Why did this happen to the greatest country in the world? How can this happen? We were all loyal patriots. Just ask George Soros (Yeah, right!). We protected everyone's rights. What went wrong? God help us! We pray to God to save us from this horrific situation and bondage. Where is God when we need Him? Who got rid of God? We should hang from trees (until they are dead) whoever eliminated God from our country, our classrooms, our government buildings, our holidays, and everything American! Yes, ironically, "*We have met the enemy, and he is us.*"[5]

---

5.   Walt Kelly, *Pogo* comic strip, Earth Day 1971.

Wake Up, America!

Remember, in June 1858, Abraham Lincoln said, "*A house divided against itself cannot stand.*" *The only way to destroy America is from within, i.e., watch out for the enemy within.* To survive in the ensuing months and years, you should do what General George S. Patton, Jr., said when he routed German Field Marshal Erwin Rommel, "*Rommel, you magnificent bastard, I read your book!*" Therefore, read this book and be prepared to fight the mother of all wars ... World War III. This is a new, different ballgame. Let us not allow the al-Qaida terrorists and other Islamo-fascists to become "*The Mouse That Roared.*"[6] Wake up, America!

> *A house divided against itself cannot stand.*
>
> **Abraham Lincoln**

> *The only way to destroy America is from within, i.e., watch out for the enemy within.*

The Mouse Trap [Al-Qaida Terrorists in Our Midst]

I received the following anonymous story, "The Mouse Trap," in one of those blast emails from a friend one day. This story reflects analogously to what is unfortunately happening in America today. It also reflects analogously to a combination of George Orwell's *Animal Farm* and Michael Savage's *The Political Zoo*. Here goes.

---

6.   The basis of the 1959 film starring Peter Sellers, this classic cold war satire-cum-parable-cum-political farce was first serialized in the *Saturday Evening Post* almost 50 years ago, appearing under the title *The Day New York Was Invaded*. At the time, the U.S. was afraid of a nuclear attack by Russia—the idea of an attack by a small country was so absurd as to seem comical. Leonard Wibberley's tiny European nation is furious about unfair US trading practices, so they send an army to invade New York City, march up Broadway, and accidentally capture the world's newest and most destructive bomb. Then they have to figure out what to do with it. A whimsical cross between Kubrick and Kafka, *The Mouse That Roared* is a quirky classic of world literature, a poignant tale of political morality, and a hilarious, ultimately triumphant portrait of international relations from the perspective of the little guy.

A mouse [The President of the US] looked through a crack in the wall [accumulated CIA intelligence] to see the farmer [Osama bin Laden] and his wife [Saddam Hussein] opening a package [their master plan]. What food [benefits to society] might it contain? He [the President] was aghast to discover that it was a mousetrap [al-Qaida terrorists]. Retreating to the farmyard [Congress of the US], the mouse [President] gave the warning: "There is a mousetrap [al-Qaida terrorists] in the house [United States]; there is a mousetrap [al-Qaida terrorists] in the house [United States]!"

The chicken [secular progressives] clucked [countered] and scratched [spun], raised her head [voice], and said, "Mr. Mouse [Mr. President], I can tell you this is a grave concern to you [all the politics you are playing], but it is of no consequence to me [no serious threat]. I cannot be bothered by it [It's the economy, stupid!]."

The mouse [President of the US] turned to the pig [liberal Democrats] and told him, "There is a mouse trap [al-Qaida terrorists] in the house [United States]." "I am so very sorry Mr. Mouse [Mr. President]," sympathized the pig [liberal Democrats], "but there is nothing I can do about it but pray [ignore it]. Rest assured, you are in my prayers [ignorance]."

The mouse [President] turned to the cow [pacifists]. She [pacifists] said, "Like wow, Mr. Mouse [Mr. President]. We have a mousetrap [al-Qaida terrorists] in our midst? I am in grave danger, no? Duh?"

Thus, the mouse [President] returned to his house [the White House], head down and dejected, to face the farmer's [Osama bin Laden's] mousetrap [al-Qaida terrorists] alone. That very night a sound [explosions] was heard throughout the house [United States], like the sound [explosions] of a mousetrap [al-Qaida terrorists] catching [blowing up] its prey [our big cities].

The farmer's wife [Saddam Hussein] rushed to see what was caught [blown up cities]. In the darkness, she [Saddam Hussein] did not see that it was a venomous snake [conservatives, Republicans, and Department of Homeland Security (DHS)] whose tail [country] the trap [al-Qaida terrorists] had caught [blown up]. The snake [conservatives, Republicans, and DHS] bit [attacked] the farmer's wife [Saddam Hussein]. The farmer [Osama bin Laden] rushed her to the hospital. She returned home with a fever. Now everyone knows you treat a fever with fresh chicken [SP] soup; so the farmer [Osama bin Laden] took his hatchet [henchmen] to the farmyard [Congress of the US] for the soup's main ingredient [SPs].

His wife's [Saddam Hussein's] sickness continued so that friends [French and Germans] and neighbors [Russians, Chinese, Iranians, Syrians, and North Koreans] came to sit with [support] her [Saddam Hussein] around the clock [in the United Nations]. To feed them, the farmer [Osama bin Laden] butchered the pig [liberal Democrats]. The farmer's wife [Saddam Hussein] did not get well. She [Saddam Hussein] died [by hanging in real life] on Saturday, December 30, 2006. So many people came to her funeral that the farmer [Osama bin Laden] had the cow [pacifists] slaughtered to provide meat for all of them to eat.

So, the next time you hear that someone is facing a problem and think that it does not concern you, remember that when the least of us [i.e., Israel] is threatened, all of us [the free world] are at risk. In the book of Genesis of *The Holy Bible*, Cain [dissenting NATO countries] said about Abel [Israel], his brother, to our God, *"Am I my brother's keeper?"* We are all involved in the "spiritual warfare [War on Terrorism]." We must all have a keen eye out [vigilance] one for another and be willing to make that extra care [sacrifice] and encouragement [support] to each other.

> ***Am I my brother's keeper?***

Yes, the SPs, liberal Democrats, and pacifists do not think seriously about the thousands of al-Qaida terrorist moles spread throughout the United States. They do not believe that these al-Qaida terrorist moles will ever affect them. Just wait until you see the first mushroom cloud from a suitcase nuclear explosion by one of them. Then, and only then, these naive people may begin to realize what a pickle we are in.

Then, and only then, we may start listening to what our President, conservatives, and Republicans are telling them regarding the threats posed by Osama bin Laden, Saddam Hussein, and their fanatical fellow travelers (extremist, left wing, radical SPs). In the meantime, they keep supporting the terrorists, Iran, North Korea, and their fellow travelers through their rhetoric and demonstrations. Everyone else sits dumb, fat, sassy, and happy. They do not realize what is in store for us in the coming months and years.

Twas the Night Before Christmas

As we experienced Christmas 2006 (Yes, Christmas, not the politically correct Holiday Season!), the song "Twas the Night Before Christmas" came to mind. I entertained these thoughts on that song:

When I read this poem, all I could think of was the clatter made by those blasted SPs and all of their spin-chatter.

They are trying to take away the freedoms we possess. If it were not for our soldiers, they would all be nothing but dead carcass.

So, all I can say is that they are very lucky, for soldiers and Santas who give them their rights to tear down this Country and put up good fights.

However, one day they will learn that freedom is not free when they all end up hanging from a huge banyan tree.

Then they are going to wish they were not such jerks for burning our flag and taking away some of our perks.

Let us counter what they do and keep them at bay, for if we only sit and watch, they will turn this country to hay.

However, when all is said and done, it will not ever matter. All their clatter and chatter will come to a splatter.

Because soldiers and Santas will continue to serve and to protect us all from their wretched words.

As I served in the Air Force for over eight years and played as Santa Claus to our kids for many years.

All I can think of is that I love our Country and will never turn it over to those traitorous SPs and their jeers.

So let us be vigilant and never let them win, or we all will be sorry and forever live in sin.

What This Book Covers

This book includes the principles, strategies, and tactics available to the Bush Administration in winning and ending the War in Afghanistan, War in Iraq, and overall War on Terrorism. *Some of the strategies and tactics addressed in this book may appear extreme to a civilized country as the United States of America.* However, we should know about and understand these strategies and tactics in the event that we must use them because we are about to be totally annihilated, conquered, and/or placed in bondage.

> *Some of the strategies and tactics addressed in this book may appear extreme to a civilized country as the United States of America.*

I have quoted much of the ideas from Sun Tzu, General George S. Patton, Jr., and Dr. Michael Savage, the greatest talk show host alive. Our Administration has made a major mistake by not learning from great warriors like Sun Tzu and General George Patton. Our Administration makes an even bigger mistake by ignoring the thoughts and ideas of Dr. Savage, a man of great intellect. All other ideas that I have not quoted from someone else are mine only. Many of the ideas are just common sense, which seem to be lacking in our politicians, Administration, and military generals. They just do not know how to fight and win an asymmetrical war. This book provides them with fresh ideas on fighting the Islamo-fascists and winning the War on Terrorism.

Therefore, if you want to know how to beat the Islamo-fascists at their own game, read this book. As the great military strategist and swordsman in Japanese history, Miyamoto Musashi, said, *"If you want to learn the craft of war, ponder over this book (meaning his book titled A Book of Five Rings). The teacher is as a needle; the disciple is as thread. You must practice constantly."*[7]

> **They just do not know how to fight and win an asymmetrical war.**

7.   Miyamoto Musashi, *A Book of Five Rings,* *"Go Rin No Sho."* Extracted on 10/13/06 from http://www.miyamotomusashi.com/gorin.htm.

Chapter 2

Pre-War Considerations

General George S. Patton, Jr. In this book, I quote extensively the sayings of General George S. Patton, Jr., because he is undoubtedly (at least in my mind) the greatest military genius and general of our modern times. General Patton was the consummate warrior. Even the German High Command believed it. We need him today. He had the gift of leadership and inspired his men to be much better than they actually were causing them to win every battle in which they fought. Appendix A of this book shows Patton's May 31, 1944, speech to the Third Army. What a motivational speech!

Where can we find another general like General George S. Patton, Jr.? Unfortunately, there is none. When he lived, General Patton was a unique leader who happened to be in the right place at the right time and under the right conditions. *World War II was made for General Patton, and General Patton was made for World War II.* Without him, we would probably all be speaking the German, Italian, and Japanese languages today.

> *World War II was made for General Patton, and General Patton was made for World War II.*

Sun Tzu. Sun Tzu said, *"Thus it is that in war the victorious strategist only seeks battle after the victory has been won, whereas he who is destined to defeat first fights and afterwards looks for victory. The consummate leader cultivates the moral law and strictly adheres to method and discipline; thus it is in his power to control success."* Appendix B of this book shows, in my opinion, the greatest political and military geniuses of all time. These great men include Sun Tzu, Niccolo Machiavelli, Miyamoto Musashi, Karl von Clausewitz, George S. Patton, Jr., Bernard Brodie, Herman Kahn, and Michael Savage.

Dr. Michael Savage. Another great living person whom I quote extensively is Dr. Michael Savage, conservative talk show host extraordinaire, who speaks his mind, cuts to the chase, and says it like it is. He calls a spade a spade. He pulls no punches. He never pussyfoots around. You know exactly what his position is and where he stands on every important issue. That is one reason why the left hates him so much, for he does not subscribe to "cutting and running" as they do. The jealous right also refuses to recognize his existence. Dr. Savage coined and invented the term "Islamo-fascists" and may be transitioning it to "Islamo-Marxist." Appendix C of this book illustrates NewsMax.com's listing of the 25 most influential talk show hosts.

War is Hell

I start from the basic premise that war is Hades. General William Tecumseh Sherman said, "*War is hell.*" Past wars have included murder, rape, plunder, pillage, torture (Far Eastern type), hatred, anger, insanity, revenge, wanton mass murder/killings, mass graves, anti-Semitism, decapitation, dismembering of bodies, cannibalism, "*man's inhumanity to man*,"[8] weapons of mass destruction (poisonous gas warfare, germ warfare, and nuclear warfare), chemical-biological-radiological (CBR) warfare, and nuclear-biological-chemical (NBC) warfare. Because of Islamo-fascist savagery, all the above have been, are, and will continue to be components of modern war and warfare. That is why war is hell.

> *War is hell.*
>
> **General William Tecumseh Sherman**

> *Never forget that men win wars.*

Men Win Wars. Remember, we are not fighting a conventional war. We are fighting a war that requires 7th Century thinking and acting. The enemy we fight uses strategies and tactics dating back to the Stone Age, Biblical Times, and/or Dark Ages. Hence, we must use ancient strategies and tactics to counter the enemy's ancient strategies and tactics. Further, we have the advantage of using better, higher-technology equipment. However, we must never forget General Patton's comment when

---

8.   Robert Burns, Poet Laureate of Scotland, said, "Man's inhumanity to man makes countless thousands mourn." Quoted from his book titled *Man Was Made to Mourn*.

he said, "*Wars may be fought with weapons, but they are won by men.*" Never forget that men win wars.

We may bomb the living daylights out of a country with our Air Force and Navy, but we must send our Army soldiers/infantry and US Marines in there (on land) to capture and conquer the real estate. We cannot plant the American flag in the air. We cannot plant the American flag on the ocean. We plant it on land as we did on the island of Iwo Jima and on the moon. President Ronald Reagan said, "*No arsenal, or no weapon in the arsenals of the world, is so formidable as the will and moral courage of free men and women.*"[9]

Politicians and Military Brass are Supreme Experts on War, Yet They Know Nothing. I wrote this book because our politicians and military brass really have had a long enough time to fight and win the wars in Afghanistan and Iraq as well as the overall War on Terror. They simply do not know how to win. This is because of what General George S. Patton said, "*Many soldiers are led to faulty ideas of war by knowing too much about too little.*"

Our politicians and military leaders know everything about warfare, yet they know nothing. They have reached the mathematical limit of the meaning of an "expert," i.e., *an expert is a person who knows more and more about less and less until finally, in the limit, he/she knows everything about nothing.*

> *An expert is a person who knows more and more about less and less until finally, in the limit, he/she knows everything about nothing.*

How to Win

If they want to learn how to win, all they need to do is to read and follow about what Sun Tzu said, which goes as follows: "*Thus we may know that there are five essentials for victory:*

(1) He will win who knows when to fight and when not to fight.
(2) He will win who knows how to handle both superior and inferior forces.

---

9. "Ronald Reagan's Wisdom," extracted on 9/27/06 from http://www.newsmax.com, Riviera Beach: Florida, 2006.

(3) He will win whose army is animated by the same spirit throughout all its ranks.

(4) He will win who, prepared himself, waits to take the enemy unprepared.

(5) He will win who has military capacity and is not interfered with by the sovereign."[10]

Note the key phrase: " ... is not interfered with by the sovereign." The sovereign in the United States consists of the president and all of his advisors (including Congress). In other words, *turn the war over to the generals, give them the single mandate to win, provide them with the necessary resources to win, stay out of their way, and let them go win the war.* That's it! Simple! Prussian military strategist, General Karl von Clausewitz, said, *"Pursue one great decisive aim with force and determination."*[11] Unfortunately, our idiotic politicians cannot accept

> ***Turn the war over to the generals, give them the single mandate to win, provide them with the necessary resources to win, stay out of their way, and let them go win the war.***

these wise counsel by two great military strategists on warfare. Mark Twain said, *"Suppose you were an idiot, and suppose you were a member of Congress. But then I repeat myself."*[12]

Generals are Puppets. Only by winning do we demonstrate our true knowledge of 21st Century warfare. As an aside, I firmly do believe that our generals now fighting the war are impotent and ineffective mainly because they are puppets of our politicians. This cannot and must not stand! It must really be frustrating for our modern-day generals to fight wars with their hands tied behind their backs!

---

10. Sun Tzu, *The Art of War*. Extracted on 10/15/06 from The Internet Classics Archive of the Massachusetts Institute of Technology at URL: http://classics.mit.edu/Tzu/artwar.html.

11. Karl von Clausewitz, *On War*. Extracted on 12/10/06 from Clausewitz Quotes/Quotations at URL: http://www.military-quotes.com/Clausewitz.htm.

12. Mark Twain, Laughing Matters. Extracted on 12/24/06 from URL: http://www.laughingmattersink.com/.

What is Asynchronous and Asymmetrical Warfare?

Combating Terrorism. Asynchronous warfare is combating terrorism. Guerrilla warfare, paramilitary warfare, and insurgent warfare are all forms of asymmetrical warfare … and so is combating terrorism. Hence, asymmetrical warfare and asynchronous warfare are the same. World War III is going to be, if it not already is, an asymmetrical or asynchronous war. It is a war of ideology, a war of philosophy, a war of culture, and a war of the survival of the Western way of life.

Contrasting Ideologies, Philosophies, and Cultures. When I talk about a war of ideology, a war of philosophy, a war of culture, and a war of the survival of the Western way of life, I am refer-
ring to the vastly contrasting ideologies, philosophies, cultures, and ways of life between the Islamo-fascists (terrorists) and the civilized world (i. e., Western society). If we did not have such a vastly different view of these things, we would not have the resulting conflict.

> *A leader is a man who can adapt principles to circumstances.*
>
> Gen. George S. Patton, Jr.

Principles of Asymmetrical Warfare. From this premise, I have devised certain principles of asymmetrical warfare that demonstrate how to beat the Islamo-fascists at their own game. If these principles are taken seriously by our political and military leaders, we will win all future asymmetrical or asynchronous wars. These principles of asymmetrical warfare were not derived from deep study, military doctrine, or complex military theories. I derived these principles from simple common sense and from the ideas expounded by my greatest modern military hero, General George S. Patton, Jr., who said, *"A leader is a man who can adapt principles to circumstances."* The principles are what you will find in this book. The circumstances are asymmetrical warfare.

Synchronous or Symmetrical Warfare. Synchronous or symmetrical warfare is *conventional* warfare. Asynchronous or asymmetrical warfare is *unconventional* warfare. Conventional warfare is what we fought in World War I, World War II, and the Korean War. Unconventional warfare is what we fought in the Vietnam War, War in Afghanistan, War in Iraq, and now the overall War on Terrorism. Therefore, *not all warfare is asymmetrical warfare.*

Characteristics of Conventional Warfare. I fully understand that misunderstandings and confusion can result when people cannot agree on the definition of words that they use in their discussions. For example, take "conventional," "synchronous," or "symmetrical" warfare. I designated WW I, WW II, and the Korean War as "conventional," "synchronous," or "symmetrical" warfare because they possess following characteristics:

> ## *Not all warfare is asymmetrical warfare.*

- The combatants on each side wore military uniforms with military insignia on them.

- Each side was signatory to the Geneva Convention.

- Each side followed a clear chain-of-command from top to bottom.

- Both sides used advanced weapons and tactics.

- There is a battlefront and lines separate the enemy from friendly forces.

If anyone would say that no war was "conventional," then we cannot discuss intelligently between conventional and unconventional warfare. I have defined what I mean by conventional warfare, and if one cannot accept and/or disregards my definition and insists that no war is "conventional," then there cannot be further logical discussion about conventional and unconventional warfare.

Characteristics of Unconventional Warfare. Whereas, for "unconventional," "asynchronous," or "unsymmetrical" warfare, there is a significant difference in what one side (the terrorists, for example) uses and the other side (the West) uses in the way of weapons, tactics, uniforms, adhering to the Geneva Convention, lines of authority, and battle lines. Here are the differences:

- **Uniforms.** The terrorists do not use a consistent uniform. You cannot differentiate the terrorists' uniforms from those of ordinary Arab-Muslim-Islamite (AMI) civilians.

- **Geneva Convention.** They do not follow the Geneva Convention.

- **Collateral Damage.** They are intentionally indiscriminate as to who they kill. They could not care less about *collateral damage* except when they charge the American military with committing collateral damage on their civilians.

- **Fratricide.** They do not even care about *fratricide* of their own people, particularly when they use them as human shields.

- **Genocide.** They believe in and practice *genocide* of the Jews and the entire Western civilization.

- **Urban Warfare.** Finally, urban warfare lends not itself to battlefronts or battle lines.

Exhaust All Alternatives before Going to War

Do not go to war except as THE last resort. All avenues of social, diplomatic, political, and economic alternatives should be exhaustively applied and proven to be unsuccessful before the military alternative should ever be employed. Of course, if we are directly attacked, all bets are off. *If attacked, we should automatically go to war.* The following is a description of each of these alternatives:

> *Do not go to war except as THE last resort.*

- **Social alternative**—International exchange programs, sister cities, Red Cross, Peace Corps, social outcasts, and international pariahs.

- **Diplomatic alternative**—Communications, discussions, understanding, disagreements, compromise, mutual respect, statesmanship, resolutions, and the United Nations (UN)

- **Political alternative**—Alliances, allies, pacts, coalitions, agreements, treaties, North Atlantic Treaty Organization (NATO), summits, declarations, and proclamations

> *If attacked, we should automatically go to war.*

- **Economic alternative**—Trade embargos, trade restrictions, blockades, and freezing of bank funds. An example of this approach is competing with the Union of Soviet Socialist Republics (USSR) in the Arms Race causing the Soviets to outspend their ability to generate the funds to pay for the arms. In the end, the USSR, now called Commonwealth of Independent States (CIS), imploded economically because the Soviets could not keep up with the United States (US) on developing the Strategic Defense Initiative (SDI) or "Star Wars" system and countering that threat. Hence, that ended the Cold War. Regarding the Cold War, Ronald Reagan said, *"Here's my strategy on the Cold War: We win; they lose."*[13]

- **Military alternative**—open clashes/conflicts, low-intensity conflicts (LIC), wars, warfare, injuries, killings, battles, destruction, weapons of mass destruction (WMDs), tactical nuclear warfare, massive retaliation, nuclear exchanges, nuclear apocalypse, mutually assured destruction (MAD), scorched-earth policy, annihilation, eradication, liquidation, and Armageddon.

International Cooperation

All avenues of international cooperation (diplomatic, political, and economic) should be attempted to achieve a peaceful end to the problem. In dealing with Islamo-fascists, the following should be considered:

- **Arresting Suspected Terrorists**—Motivate other countries to assist in seeking and arresting suspected Islamo-fascists and bring them swiftly to justice. Extradite to the US those Islamo-fascists who committed terrorist crimes in the US but were captured in other countries.

- **United International Front**—Team with all of the nations in the world that are on our side to go after Islamo-fascists in a united front. *Nations are either for or against terrorism.* Their actions show on which side of the line they stand. Do not listen to their words. Observe their actions.

- **International Anti-Islamo-fascist Force**—Establish a joint international anti-Islamo-fascist force headed by the USA. Membership should be limited only to nations that support the US 100 percent and that we know for a fact that they support us. Countries on the caliber of England, Japan, Canada, South Korea, Australia, Philippines, Germany (maybe), and so on should be part of this force. When a country commits and deploys

> ***Nations are either for or against terrorism.***

---

13.   "Ronald Reagan's Wisdom," extracted on 9/27/06 from the following URL: http://www.newsmax.com, Riviera Beach: Florida, 2006.

military forces and funds to combat Islamo-fascists, that action proves that they are behind the USA 100 percent.

- **Resource Denial**—Deny money, support, and safe sanctuary to Islamo-fascists. Accomplish this through freezing their bank accounts, eliminating their funding sources, and eliminating those governments that provide them with support and sanctuary. You are either for us or against us. There will be no "willful financing" of Islamo-fascists. We must make other nations deny "safe haven" to Islamo-fascists. If they do not, they shall face harsh consequences … and then follow through. Do not just give lip service.

Declaration of War

Know Where Each Elected Official Stands. *Never go to war without an official declaration of war from Congress.* These declarations should normally be for worldwide wars (e.g., World War I, World War II, and the imminent World War III). All Congressmen should show whether they are *"for us or against us"*[14] in a recorded, documented vote. We must know where each elected official stands.

US Declared War on Countries That Did Not Attack Us. Japan killed over 2,400 Americans when they attacked Pearl Harbor on December 7, 1941. The United States declared war on Imperialist Japan. Shortly thereafter, the United States also declared war on Nazi Germany and Fascist Italy. Germany and Italy did not attack America as Japan did, yet Congress declared war on them anyway. Is that not strange?

> *Never go to war without an official declaration from Congress.*

Al-Qaida Gets a Pass. However, the US did not declare war on al-Qaida (In the press, this term is also spelled as al Qaida, Al Qaida, al-Qaeda, al Qaeda, or Al Qaeda.) when it directly attacked the World Trade Center Twin Towers in New York and killed almost 3,000 people in that heinous attack (The 3,000 includes deaths at the Pentagon and Shanksville, Pennsylvania.). *Is it not strange that we give al-Qaida a pass just because it is a pseudo-military organization instead of a country or nation?*

---

14. Shortly after 9/11/01, President Bush declared to the world's nations, "You're either for us or against us." Our politicians should be subjected to the same test.

Sidebar Comments

Business in Saudi Arabia. Regarding different spellings of the same name or terms, I remember when I had worked at The Titan Corporation and did some work for one of Titan's divisions called Titan SureBeam (now defunct), the problem of different name spellings came to my attention. At the time, we were dealing with businesses in Saudi Arabia to provide them with SureBeam systems for electronic pasteurization that killed harmful bacteria instantly, enhancing a food's quality, and extending its shelf life without changing its taste or texture. Similar to a microwave oven, the SureBeam system used ordinary electricity as its energy source to pasteurize food after it was processed and packaged.

> *Is it not strange that we give al-Qaida a pass just because it is a pseudo-military organization instead of a country or nation?*

Different Spelling of Names Did Not Matter. At any rate, I had received a letter from our Saudi Arabian representative who was located in Saudi Arabia. I noticed that this fellow had his name spelled two different ways on the same page of the letter. In a phone conversation with him, I asked him, "Which was the correctly spelled name?" He said, "Either way; it didn't matter." I was floored. How can a person's name be so trivial and unimportant to him that he didn't care how it was spelled even if it is spelled two different ways on the same piece of correspondence! Needless to say, I was flabbergasted.

Motive Makes the Difference. Now, five years later, I begin to have a better understanding of why it would not matter to a Middle Easterner as to how he spells his name. If you do not want to be easily recognized, identified, and found, you would not mind spelling you name differently. If you had something to hide, you would not mind creating confusion with your name. If you were doing something illegal, immoral, or unethical, you would want to have aliases, faked names, or multiple ways of spelling your name.

Strategy of Confusion. Take this simple, common name for example: Muhammad, Muhammed, Mohammad, Mohammed, Muhamad, Muhamed, Mohamad, Mohamed, and Mahomet. *There are nine known different ways to spell that same name!* So, if you did a different spelling of your name with your first name, middle name, and surname, there would be no way to recognize your correct name in a humungous database. There would be a gargantuan number of combinations of your first, middle, and last names together. Nobody could determine who you are! Wow, what a strategy! Appendix D of this book shows numerous ways various Arabic words and names are spelled. They confuse everyone.

> *There are nine different ways to spell that same name!*

Many Ways to Spell My Name. Hence, from now on, I am going to spell my first name as Robert, Roberto, Rob, Robbo, Robby, Bert, Bob, Bobby, and Bobbo. I'll have nine first names too! I will also spell my middle name as Takeo, Take, Take-bo, and Tak. Furthermore, I will spell my last name as Uda, Euda, Ooda, Oowda, Ouda, Uuda, Yewda, Yoda, Yuda, and Youda. I'll have 10 different last names! I'm even one better than Muhammad. How great it is!

Keep All of Our Government Agencies Confused. Now, if I combine them together with three different combinations of first, middle, and last names, nobody will ever be able to find the correct Robert Uda or Bob Uda … particularly if I use different spellings and combinations of names in the same piece of correspondence! Won't that put the police department, Department of Motor Vehicles (DMV), Social Security Administration (SSA), Internal Revenue Service (IRS), Federal Bureau of Investigation (FBI), Central Intelligence Agency (CIA), and National Security Agency (NSA) all in a tizzy? That's what the terrorists are doing to them!

A Great Problem for Genealogists. It is no wonder the genealogists or family history researchers have a heck of a time sorting out the correct names of people. With that variety of names for the same person, it could give a genealogist a constant, severe migraine headache. However, for some reason or other, when these genealogists get hooked on performing that kind of research, they do it forever. I give them a lot of credit for persevering through all of that, I'm sure, frustration.

We Must Remember the Lessons Learned from the Vietnam War

Robert McNamara's 11 Lessons from Vietnam. Secretary of Defense Robert McNamara badly screwed up running the Vietnam War, and he later apologized for it. Through all of his misjudgments and mistakes, he did learn a few lessons, which we should not ignore and repeat in our current and future wars. Remember, it was George Santayana, who said "*Those who cannot remember the past are condemned to repeat it.*"[15] Robert McNamara's 11 lessons from Vietnam are as follows:

> ***Those who cannot remember the past are condemned to repeat it.***
>
> **George Santayana**

1.   *We misjudged then—and we have since—the geopolitical intentions of our adversaries ... and we exaggerated the dangers to the United States of their actions.*

2.   *We viewed the people and leaders of South Vietnam in terms of our own experience. We totally misjudged the political forces within the country.*

3.   *We underestimated the power of nationalism to motivate a people to fight and die for their beliefs and values.*

4.   *Our judgments of friend and foe alike reflected our profound ignorance of the history, culture, and politics of the people in the area, and the personalities and habits of their leaders.*

5.   *We failed then—and have since—to recognize the limitations of modern, high-technology military equipment, forces, and doctrine.*

6.   *We failed as well to adapt our military tactics to the task of winning the hearts and minds of people from a totally different culture.*

7.   *We failed to draw Congress and the American people into a full and frank discussion and debate of the pros and cons of a large-scale military involvement ... before we initiated the action.*

8.   *After the action got under way and unanticipated events forced us off our planned course, we did not fully explain what was happening and why we were doing what we did.*

9.   *We did not recognize that neither our people nor our leaders are omniscient. Our judgment of what is in another people's or country's best interest should*

---

15.   George Santayana (16 December 1863 in Madrid, Spain—26 September 1952 in Rome, Italy), was a philosopher, essayist, poet, and novelist. Taken from *Reason in Common Sense*, the first volume of his *The Life of Reason*.

be put to the test of open discussion in international forums. We do not have the God-given right to shape every nation in our image or as we choose.

10. *We did not hold to the principle that U.S. military action ... should be carried out only in conjunction with multinational forces supported fully (and not merely cosmetically) by the international community.*

11. *We failed to recognize that in international affairs, as in other aspects of life, there might be problems for which there are no immediate solutions. At times, we may have to live with an imperfect, untidy world.*

Underlying many of these errors lay our failure to organize the top echelons of the executive branch to deal effectively with the extraordinarily complex range of political and military issues.[16]

> ### We do not have the God-given right to shape every nation in our image or as we choose.
>
> **Robert McNamara**

We Did Not Learn Our Lessons from Vietnam. *Already, it is obvious that we do not learn our lessons of past wars.* In Iraq and Afghanistan, we are violating every one of these 11 costly lessons learned in the Vietnam War. Sad!

Our Leaders Do Not Know How to Fight and Win. Sun Tzu said, "*If you know the enemy and know yourself, you need not fear the result of a hundred battles. If you know yourself but not the enemy, for every victory gained you will also suffer a defeat. If you know neither the enemy nor yourself, you will succumb in every battle.*"[17] This is why we lost in Vietnam. We did not know how to fight to win that war ... much less know the enemy and ourselves. We made an ingenious initial entry into both the Afghanistan and Iraq wars. However, since then, we reverted to a Vietnam *modus operandi*. This is why we

> ### Already, it is obvious that we do not learn our lessons of past wars.

---

16. Bonnie Azab Powell, "Robert McNamara, Errol Morris return to Berkeley to share lessons learned from 'Fog of War'," *UC Berkeley News*, 05 February 2004. The 11 lessons in this article were cited from *Globe and Mail*, January 24, 2004, issue.

17. Sun Tzu, *The Art of War*. Extracted on 10/15/06 from The Internet Classics Archive of the Massachusetts Institute of Technology at URL: http://classics.mit.edu/Tzu/artwar.html.

are now losing in Afghanistan and Iraq. When are we going to listen to Sun Tzu and win these wars?

Chapter 3

Going to War

Congress People and Their Children Go First

Politicians' Children Drafted First. If Congress declares war, the sons and daughters of all of these politicians should be drafted first and sent to the battlefront to fight in the war. *Make this a matter of federal law.* That requirement should have a definite impact on whether they would really want the United States to go to war or not.

> *Make this a matter of federal law.*

Politicians should Personally Lead the Battles. Furthermore, all elected politicians should be suited up in military gear and placed at the battlefront of all wars into which they send our war fighters. *Again, make this a matter of federal law.* In past wars, the true leaders were out in front of the army leading the war-fighters into battle. For example, we had the following great American leaders leading the fight in their respective wars or battles:

- Daniel Boone, a great frontiersman who never shied away from a fight during the 1760s-1770s

- General George Washington crossing the Delaware River in the Battle of Trenton during the Revolutionary War, 1776

- Tecumseh (Shawnee), brigadier general under the British at the Battle of the Thames, where he lost his life, during the War of 1812

- Davy Crockett on his last stand at the Alamo, 1836

- Union Admiral David Glasgow Farragut ("Old Salamander") at Mobile Bay during the Civil War said, "*Damn the torpedoes! Full speed ahead!*", 1864

- Geronimo (Apache), most legendary and feared of all Apache warriors in Arizona during the 1850s—1880s

- General George A. Custer's last stand at the Battle of the Little Big Horn, 1876

- Sitting Bull (Sioux) defeats General Custer at the Battle of the Little Big Horn, 1876

- Lt. Colonel Theodore Roosevelt and the Rough Riders in the Battle at San Juan Hill during the Spanish-American War, 1898

- Lt Audie Murphy, the most decorated US soldier in WW II with 33 awards and decorations including the Medal of Honor, credited for killing over 240 of the enemy, wounded three times, fought in nine major campaigns across the European Theater, and survived the war, 1943-45

- General A.C. McAuliffe, commander of 101st Airborne Division, when the German's asked him to surrender Bastogne during the Battle of Bastogne, said, "*Nuts!*", 1944

- General George S. Patton, Jr., and his Third Army's drive into Germany, which helped end WW II, 1945

Leading Battles should be an Eternal Principle. Whatever happened to leaders like these? *Leading battles should be an eternal principle to keep our errant politicians from starting frivolous wars.* I would love to have seen President Lyndon Banes Johnson and Secretary of Defense Robert McNamara leading the various battles in Southeast Asia fighting their way through the Vietnamese jungles. Watching President Bill Clinton on national television leading the charge in all of the silly wars he started in foreign lands would have been a real gas indeed! It would have been like watching losing presidential candidate Governor Michael

> *Leading battles should be an eternal principle to keep our errant politicians from starting frivolous wars.*

Dukakis riding in that tank with helmet on in that nationally televised campaign commercial. In that way, we will see how badly they and our Congress people will ever want to go to war in the future.

We Need Real Generals Today. We need General Patton today in Afghanistan and Iraq. We need him to "kick the rears" of the Iranians and North Koreans. Where is General Patton who wanted to attack the Russians after the close of WW

II? Where is General Douglas MacArthur who wanted to cross the Yalu River to attack the Red Chinese during the Korean Conflict? Where are these "old blood and guts" generals today? Unfortunately, there is none. General Wesley Clark presents a real joke of an example (learn all about General Wesley Clark by going to this URL: http://www.zpub.com/un/clark.html).

Go to War to Win

War is Avenue of Last Resort. Going to war should be the avenue of last resort. However, once we make a majority decision to go to war, do not hesitate, do not flinch, do not look back, do not have cold feet, do not have "buyer's remorse," and do not speak out against it. Move forward with great vigor. *Never go to war unless you go to war to win. The objectives of winning the war should be for the survival of the country, survival of our citizens, and survival of our way of life.*

> ***Never go to war unless you go to war to win. The objectives of winning the war should be for the survival of the country, survival of our citizens, and survival of our way of life.***

When Attacked, Quickly Declare War. Whenever any enemy attacks us on our homeland, we should quickly declare war and go to war immediately thereafter. Attacks on Pearl Harbor on December 7, 1941, and the World Trade Center and Pentagon on September 11, 2001, are valid reasons for declaring and going to war against the attackers. We did it correctly after the Pearl Harbor attack, but we became wimp-outs after 9/11. No attack on our homeland should ever go without a quick, devastating, retaliatory response. If not, our enemies will perceive us as weak (as they currently do) and will repeatedly attack us in the future.

War of Attrition

A Flawed Strategy. General William Westmoreland, commander of U.S. Forces in Vietnam, coined the phrase "war of attrition." His central strategy to fight this "war of attrition" was somewhat flawed. Westmoreland's objective was to decimate the North Vietnamese people "to the point of national disaster for generations to come," while in South Vietnam, his aim was to eliminate Viet Cong (VC) combatants faster than they could be replenished.[18]

Meat Grinder and Search & Destroy Strategies. The goal simply was to pound the enemy into submission. The Pentagon called this strategy the "meat grinder," which was supposed to be achieved through massive bombing of North Vietnam and "search-and-destroy" missions in the south that would root out the National Liberation Front (NLF) and eradicate them with US air power. The hope was that this strategy would buy time for the Saigon government to become a viable political and military entity.[19]

Discard War of Attrition Strategy. Never take the "war of attrition" approach. That was foolishly done in Vietnam. Now, the wars in Afghanistan and Iraq, although started out correctly, are being transitioned into wars of attrition. The war of attrition suppose to meat grind down the enemy forces. However, this "war of attrition" in Afghanistan and Iraq grinds down our own soldiers … one soldier at a time. You do not want a war of attrition to go that way. The American public will not stand for it. So, *either turn those wars over totally to the generals or get our troops out of there!* Fighting those wars the way we are doing today is both ludicrous and insane.

Let the Generals Run the War

Turn It Over to the Generals. When we go to war, we should turn it over to the generals to run. Generals have been trained to fight and win wars. Do not use them as puppets to perform for politicians as puppeteers holding onto the strings. Do not tie one of their arms behind their backs and expect them to win the fight. Give them all the resources, latitude, authority, and power to wage and win the war. If you are not willing to do that, then do not go to war in the first place!

Only Order is to Go Win the War. Sun Tzu said, "In war, the general receives his commands from the sovereign." In the United States, the sovereign is the president or the commander-in-chief.

> *Either turn those wars over totally to the generals or get our troops our of there!*

---

18. Michael Bilton and Kevin Sim, *Four Hours in My Lai* (New York: Penguin Books, 1992), p. 32.

19. Ibid.

However, in today's environment, the president should give only one command to the general or, in our case, the Chairman of the Joint Chiefs of Staff. That command is this: "*Go win the war by any means possible.*" That is it! Let the Joint Chiefs of Staff figure out what to do and how to win the war. All politicians should stay out of their way and let them do their job the best way they know how to do it. If they do not win the war in 12 months, replace them with

> **Go win the war by any means possible.**

better generals who can and will accomplish the mission in the shortest time possible.

Politicians Stay Out of It!

Vietnam War. No politician or politicians should be involved in directing the war. Keep them out of it! They are the ones who have screwed up past wars and got our war-fighters unnecessarily killed by the tens and hundreds of thousands. Presidents Kennedy and Johnson screwed up the Vietnam War. President Ford had to take the retreat tactic, pull out, and lose the Vietnam War. *The Vietnam War unnecessarily killed over 47,000 war fighters. What a waste of valuable human life!*

World War II. President Truman made the right decision to drop the atomic bomb on Hiroshima and Nagasaki, which ended the war in the Pacific. However, President Truman made the mistake of stopping General George S. Patton, Jr., from fighting the Russians as Patton had desired. He also made the mistake of stopping General Douglas MacArthur from taking our troops across the Yalu River and attacking the Red Chinese. If Truman had allowed

> **The Vietnam War unnecessarily killed over 47,000 war fighters. What a waste of valuable human life!**

those two generals to run things as they should have, we would not have had the frapping Cold War!

Afghan and Iraq Wars. President George W. Bush has made the wrong decision in fighting the Afghan War and Iraq War as was done in Vietnam. He started these wars correctly with carpet bombing and massive force. However, as time went on, we turned wimpy. We should have wiped out all insurgents when we had the chance. Instead, we are now experiencing another "war of attrition" of our troops!

Turn Wars Over to the Generals. President Bush should turn over to the generals (i.e., Joint Chiefs of Staff) the wars in Afghanistan and Iraq and personally stay out of it. Let them fight and win those wars and then bring our troops home where they belong. Whatever it takes to win those wars should be taken. General George S. Patton said, "*Sure, we want to go home. We want this war over with. The quickest way to get it over with is to go get the bastards who started it.*"

Fight to Win the War on Terrorism. It is no wonder the Democrats and SPs are dead against these wars as well as the "War on Terrorism." It is no wonder the North Koreans are spitting in our collective faces. It is no wonder the Iranians are scoffing at the UN resolutions and badmouthing the US. It is no wonder we are having all kinds of terrorist acts being committed all over the world. If we are going to fight a war on terror, let us fight to WIN the War on Terror!

War is Against People

When you fight a war, you fight people. You cannot effectively wage a war and win when you fight against an idea, an ideology, a concept, an "-ism," an inanimate object, land, an infrastructure, animals, plants, and any other such ridiculous things. In other words, *you cannot fight and win a war against drugs, against poverty, or against terrorism.* There will be no end to them unless and until we change our paradigm to make them a war on specific people … the bad guys.

> *You cannot fight and win a war against drugs, against poverty, or against terrorism.*

War on Drugs. The War on Drugs continues on and never seems to have an end or conclusion. Until we change the War on Drugs to the War on Drug Dealers, War on Drug Pushers, War on Drug Addicts, War on Drug Cartels, War on Drug Traffickers, or War on Drug Smugglers, nothing positive will happen to win that war. You win the War on Drugs only when you knock off (one-by-one) all those who are illicitly participating in advancing the sale of drugs for money.

War on Poverty. Likewise, the War on Poverty rages on for years and years, and there is no end in sight. The War on Poverty will always exist until we change its designation to one or more of the following:

- War for Educating Poor People
- War on Those Who Attempt to Keep Poor People on the Figurative Plantation
- War on Extreme Left-Wing SPs Who Advance Hand-out (Entitlement) Programs

We Can Never Win the War on Poverty. By definition, you cannot eradicate poverty. As long as we have the rich, we will always have the poor. As long as we have the "haves," we will have the "have-nots." Hence, by definition, we will never eliminate the poor. However, we can make things better for the poor by educating them, increasing the overall economic pie, and outlawing those who attempt to keep the poor on the figurative plantation.

War on Terrorism. The same argument applies to the War on Terror. It is no different with the War on Terrorism. We must change that paradigm to the War on Terrorists, War with al-Qaida, War with the Taliban, War with Hezbollah, War with Hamas, and/or War on Islamo-fascists. You need not fight a country or nation to go to war. We can go to war with an organization, a group of people, and members of an ideological party. We need to start knocking off Islamo-fascists one by one until our work is done. These groups represent a finite number of human bodies.

One at a Time

Our poodle dogs do not have any fleas because we have killed them one flea at a time. Terrorists are no different than fleas. We just need to knock them off one terrorist at a time. In addition, we don't need to make any fanfare about it either. We just snuff them out quietly, deliberately, and consistently. Finally, one day, we will get up, and there will be no terrorists (or fleas) left. Isn't that too bad!

> *Terrorists are no different than fleas. We just need to knock them off one terrorist at a time.*

World War III?

We do not need to call the War on Islamo-fascists as World War III. We do not need to call it as we did the Korean War, Vietnam War, or Gulf War. *Unless we went to war with Iran, we don't need to go to war with a country.* We simply can go to war with a group of people such as al-Qaida, Taliban, Hezbollah, Hamas, or Islamo-fascists.

> *Unless we went to war with Iran, we don't need to go to war with a country.*

Chapter 4

Dealing with Isfasts

Before we go any further, we must define what we mean by "Islamo-fascists." I call them *Isfasts* for short. Isfasts are comprised of a smaller percentage of all Arabs, Muslims, and Islamites (AMIs) in the world. The Isfasts attacked the United States on September 11, 2001, destroyed the World Trade Center Twin Towers, and killed nearly 3,000 innocent non-combatant civilians in the process.

Hijacking of the Islamic Religion. The Isfasts want to wipe Israel off the face of the map. They desire to kill all infidels (i.e., Americans, Westerners, and the non-believers of the Islamic religion). *They hijacked the Islamic religion and twisted the passages of the Quran* (In the literature, this is also spelled Qur'an, Quraan, Koran, Koraan, Qoraan, or Qoran) *to support their own ends.* They celebrated and danced in the streets when the Twin Towers came down. They include the nations and people that finance and support the terrorists. They want to dominate the world.

Who Comprise the Isfasts. The Isfasts comprise about 10 percent of the AMI population of the world. Since there are approximately 1 billion

> *They hijacked the Islamic religion and twisted the passages of the Quran to support their own ends.*

of these people, the Isfasts is comprised of about 100 million people. This is a conservative estimate. Some have this figure up to 150 million people. That is half the population of the United States. The Isfasts include the members of al-Qaida, Taliban, Hezbollah, Hamas, and the anti-American peoples of Iran, Syria, Saudi Arabia, Egypt, and other Middle Eastern, East Asian, and Pacific Rim countries that believe in and expound the goal of "Death to America." That is a formidable group with which to contend.

Who the Isfasts are Not. The Isfasts do not include the approximately 90 percent of all AMIs in the world who are peace loving and tolerant of other religions and peoples of the world. President George W. Bush said, *"Islam is peace, and the United States is not against the religion of Islam, but those who pervert the religion to support terrorism and mass murder."*[20]

What Motivates the Isfasts?

The Isfasts want power, control, dominance, and money, not to mention 72 virgins when they depart this life. They desire to kill all Americans, British, Israelis, Christians (infidels), and unbelievers of Islam. Hence, we must terminate all Isfast terrorists. They are insane, fanatical, committed, and vicious. They do not fear death or dying. Indeed, they will gladly go on insane human suicide missions just to kill the infidels and earn their 72 virgins in their twisted version of the hereafter. *Their motto is simple: Either you convert to Islam or you die.* That is some religion; is it not?

> *Their motto is simple: Either you convert to Islam or you die.*

Food for Thought

Duty to Kill All Infidels. I once heard a supposed expert on Muslims and the Quran (also Koran), which is the Muslims' book of scripture of the Prophet Muhammad's instructions received from Allah. This expert was a guest on the Michael Savage talk radio show. This guest had said some things that, if true, are quite disturbing and unnerving. He read translated verses from the Quran to the effect that Muslims have a duty to kill all infidels (defined as all Christians) until the last one is gone from the entire world. Then, their faith will have peace and be peaceful because there will be nobody alive who would be against their religion.

Kill, Burn, Mutilate, and Hang. Another scary set of verses that he read said that it was okay for Muslims to kill infidels, chop off their body parts, burn

---

20.   Jim Garamone, "Islam Growing in America, U.S. Military," *American Forces Information Service News Articles*, *DefenseLINK News*, October 4, 2001. Extracted on 9/5/06 from the following URL: http://www.defenselink.mil/news/Oct2001/n10042001_200110043.html.

them, and hang them. The Isfasts did these four things to the American civilian contractors that they killed in Iraq, i.e., the Isfasts killed, burned, mutilated, and hanged these contractors on a bridge in Baghdad.

Beheading of a South Korean Hostage. Additionally, the Muslim extremists had kidnapped and held a South Korean, Kim Sun-Il, as a hostage who they had threatened on national television to kill and burn if South Korea deployed their troops to Iraq. They beheaded that South Korean hostage and dumping his body alongside a road. Animals! In spite of that disgusting slaughter, South Korea still deployed their troops to Iraq. These extremist, radical Isfasts claim to be carrying out instructions from the Quran.

AMI Hypocrites Killed. According to the extremist, radical Muslims, the mainstream AMIs who disobey the instructions in the Quran are considered hypocrites and are subject to being killed by them (Isfasts) that obey the Quran. Obviously, this accounts for the thousands upon thousands of good AMIs who have been murdered and buried in mass graves in Iraq and other Middle Eastern countries. Additionally, honor killings by relatives, often are either ignored or only lightly punished by authorities, are also commonplace in the Middle East.

Enemy in Our Midst. It was surmised that that could be the reason why those hundreds of thousands of AMIs living in the United States do not speak out against the terrible acts of the extremist, radical Muslim terrorists. Many AMIs are afraid of retribution. However, many in our midst also support the Isfast terrorists. *The enemy is in our midst, folks, and the extremist, radical, left wing SPs in this country and abroad support them.*

> *The enemy is in our midst, folks, and the extremist, radical, left wing SPs in this country and abroad support them.*

Muhammad. He pointed out verses in the Quran that stated that Muhammad had a Christian wife. Muhammad wrote about himself being what is defined in today's language as a pedophile, a killer, and a philanderer. There were several other things discussed (up to 10 items), but I cannot remember all of them. Please note that I am only reporting what I believe I had heard on that radio show. I make no judgments of these allegations at this time without further study and analysis. In other words, I report; you decide.

Armageddon and World Domination. However, what I heard gave me pause for contemplation. What if the above information is true? Then what do we do? The enemy is in our midst. I hope these things are not true. However, if they are true, when the Isfast terrorists go into full action, I believe that it will be the beginning of Armageddon. If any of these fellow-traveling, extremist, radical Muslims do not like it in the United States, they should move to Iraq or some other Middle Eastern country. However, they do not need to if their ultimate goal is world domination.

The Lame-stream Media. I was reporting what I had heard on the Michael Savage radio talk show on what this guy (I cannot remember his name.) had said, a supposed expert on the Quran and Muslims. I make no judgments. I just report what I had heard; you decide. What he said really grabbed my attention and caused me to pause and think a bit as compared to the evidences of what is happening in the world. These reports never air in the mainstream media,

> *When the Isfast terrorists go into full action, I believe that it will be the beginning of Armageddon.*

which is mostly SP and thus supports and promotes the SP agenda. This is why Michael Savage calls the mainstream media the lame-stream media. That is why I never watch, listen to, or read the mainstream SP media anymore.

Study of Quran Required. If you go to http://www.ask.com and in the "Ask Jeeves" box type in the following, "Verses in the Quran that talks about killing all infidels," you will find many documents that cover this subject. I cannot verify/validate the veracity of these writings, so I reserve judgment on all of them. They may be true or false. A concerned, knowledgeable person must make a thorough study before making any rational judgments on that material.

Cleric Speaks Up. It was uplifting to see/hear on Fox News the big cleric leader in Iraq, Grand Ayatollah Ali al-Sistani. He told the troublemaker lower-level Shiite Muslim cleric, Moqtada al-Sadr (who was trying to make a name for himself), in Faluja to tone it down. Moqtada al-Sadr's followers had slaughtered, dismembered, burned, and hanged four American contractors and are now

> *We should eliminate al-Sadr by wiping out Sadr City. Why waste any more good Marines' lives?*

killing some of our Marines. *We should eliminate al-Sadr by wiping out Sadr City. Why waste any more good Marines' lives?*

More Clerics Need to Speak Up. We need more of the clerics in the Middle East and in the United States to speak up and not just to keep quiet against these Sunni and Shiite insurgents, terrorists, and al-Qaida. If the clerics would speak up instead of keeping quiet, then people would not wonder if they and their followers support the terrorists. I hope more of them start speaking up to help the situation instead of just sitting back and letting things escalate.

Sidebar Comment

I once worked for The Titan Corporation in the area of counterterrorism and antiterrorism. A Middle Eastern man living in San Diego phoned me as he was looking for employment. We had communicated several times before by email, and he was eager to come to work at Titan. However, after that phone call, I wrote in my last email to him that we were working in counterterrorism and antiterrorism. Strangely, he abruptly stopped communicating with me. At that time, I had wondered if the guy was a terrorist, but I just let it slide. However, I kept thinking about that interaction even until today … over five years later. It is just something to think about.

Understanding the Islamo-fascist Terrorist Strategy

Isfast Strategy. Listed below is how the Isfasts operate:

- *Element of Surprise*—The Islamo-fascist terrorists do what is least expected. They strike quickly (*blitzkrieg* like).

- *Big Impact*—The Islamo-fascist terrorists perform acts that make a huge impact on the population, the economy, and the psyche of the citizenry … such as 9/11.

- *Shocking*—The Islamo-fascist terrorists do things that shock us. They do the unbelievable such as beheadings on television.

- *Wide Publicity*—The Islamo-fascist terrorists perform acts that garner the widest worldwide publicity as aided by al-Jazeera and the American mainstream media/press.

- *Kill Large Numbers of People*—The Islamo-fascist terrorists perform acts that indiscriminately kill very large numbers of people in one incident (e.g., nuclear blast). They do not discriminate among who they kill … killing men, women, children, young people, old folks, the sick and afflicted, crippled people, civilians, military personnel … it does not matter to them who they kill. A kill is a kill to them.

- *Suicide Missions*—The Islamo-fascist terrorists conduct asynchronous human suicide missions (*kamikaze*-like missions such as human suicide bombers).

Mirror Their Strategy. Our strategy to combat or counter their strategy is to mirror their strategy but multiply our kill rate by an order of magnitude (i.e., 10 times more) … preferably even more, say, by 20 times more or two orders of magnitude. General George S. Patton said, "*You shouldn't underestimate an enemy, but it is just as fatal to overestimate him.*" So, let us neither underestimate nor overestimate the Isfasts, but let us, instead, eliminate ALL of them.

Queries of a Young Japanese Boy

A young boy from Japan named Hitoshi something-or-other posed the following questions on the Internet. I answered those questions. Here are the questions and my answers:

1. *Do you support taking reprisals on the terrorists?*

   Yes, I do support taking reprisals on the terrorists. Terrorism is like a cancer to the body. If you do not cut it out, burn it out, poison it, or kill it, it will eventually consume the entire body. This is not only an American problem. It is a problem for every peaceful, freedom-loving nation in the world.

   > *Terrorism is like a cancer to the body. If you do not cut it out, burn it out, poison it, or kill it, it will eventually consume the entire body.*

2. *Do you think that the terrorists would take any other actions if the 9/11 WTC attack wasn't done?*

Yes, even if the attack on the World Trade Center (WTC) did not occur, terrorists would continue their evil work as they had done previously on the WTC in 1993, Pan Am flight 103, the Marine barracks in Lebanon, the military barracks in Saudi Arabia, the American warship USS Cole, our embassies in Africa, and on and on it goes. Terrorists want to rule the world. They want to rid the world of the freedoms we currently enjoy. They consider everyone not of their ilk as infidels.

Their world domination is the same kind of thinking of Adolf Hitler of Germany, Joseph Stalin of Russia, Benito Mussolini of Italy, Hideki Tojo of Japan, and Mao Tse-Tung of Red China. It is the same thinking today of Osama bin Laden (OBL), Ayman al-Zawahiri, Mullah Omar, the captured and executed butcher of Baghdad Saddam Hussein, Hitler of Iran Mahmoud Ahmadinejad, Kim Jong Il of North Korea, the eradicated decapitating butcher Abu Musab al-Zarqawi, and others of their ilk.

3. *Do you believe that Osama bin Laden will be found and arrested?*

Yes, if OBL is not already dead, he will be found and disposed of efficiently and effectively. He is an evil man who should receive an evil man's just rewards. Having been born and raised in America, I am an American man of Japanese ancestry. I am glad to have had this opportunity to explain to you the feelings of about 90 percent of the people of the United States. I am proud to be an American and work in anti-and counterterrorism.

> *Yes, if OBL is not already dead, he will be found and disposed of efficiently and effectively. He is an evil man who should receive an evil man's just rewards.*

Difference between Terrorists and Freedom Fighters

To clarify the distorted thinking of those who portray "terrorists" as "freedom fighters," I present the correct definitions of both terms.

What is a Terrorist? A "terrorist":

- Fights to kill innocent civilians (men, women, children, old, young, infirm, everyone) for worldwide shock impact, to make a political statement, and to put fear/terror in the hearts and minds of the general populace. *The sword without, and terror within, shall destroy both the young man and the virgin* [young people and both men and women], *the suckling* [infants] *also with the man of gray hairs* [old people]. (Deut. 32:25)

- Commits murder, killings, slaughter, and mass killings.

- Is a butcher and war criminal who commits crimes to achieve evil ends.

- Uses fear motivation through terror.

- Forces their fundamentalist Muslim religion on everyone (their practice is you either convert or die by decapitation).

- Believes that their God (Allah) sanctions indiscriminate killing of people they call infidels (i.e., Westerners, Americans, Israelis, and all non-believers of Islam).

- Strives to take away our basic freedoms (particularly women's rights).

- Hates everyone (infidels) not of his/her ilk.

- Despises the free enterprise system, yet uses it to promote and achieve their ends.

- Seeks world domination.

What is a Freedom Fighter? On the other hand, a "freedom fighter":

- Fights to free those illegally held in bondage.

- Fights for people's rights to life, liberty, and the pursuit of happiness.

- Fights to protect the freedoms such as those listed in the American Bill of Rights.

- Fights for free speech.

- Tolerates the free exercise of all religions.

- Refrains from indiscriminately killing people.
- Strives for peace and prosperity.

Difference is Between Evil and Righteous Intents. How some people (particularly extremist, left wing, radical secular progressives) cannot distinguish the difference between the definitions of these two terms is way beyond me. It is very simple—one is evil and the other is righteous. People who do not or cannot see the difference are evil, mentally incapacitated, extreme radical leftists, or Islamo-fascist sympathizers. These people present a danger to the well-being of the people of the United States.

Illustration of a Radical SP Mind. To illustrate the distorted, extremist, left wing, radical, secular progressive mind, look at how one of them defines "terrorists":
- *Terrorists*—those who are trying to destabilize legitimate governments like Al Qaeda[21]

This implies that Al Qaeda is a stable, legitimate government. How absurd! Therefore, this person concludes the United States, Great Britain, and Israel are terrorist nations. Furthermore, this is how this same mind defines "freedom fighters":
- *Freedom Fighters*—those, like the Palestinians and the Iraqis, who are trying to liberate their lands from foreign occupiers.[22] This person considers the terrorists or insurgents as freedom fighters and the Israelis in Israel and the American-led coalition forces currently in Iraq as foreign occupiers.

Distorted SP Conclusion. These definitions imply that Al Qaeda, radical Shiites, radical Sunnis, Hezbollah, Hamas, Taliban, and terrorists/insurgents in Iraq, Afghanistan, Lebanon, and Palestine are all "freedom fighters." Hence, the Americans, British, and Israelis are all foreign occupiers and terrorist nations.

Liberalism is a Mental Disorder. It is no wonder that *Dr. Michael Savage calls liberalism a mental disorder!* This is the reason why normal people cannot

---

21. John WorldPeace, "THE WORLDPEACE JOURNAL: a personal perspective of current events," *The WorldPeace Peace Page*. Extracted on 9/18/06 from URL http://www.johnworld-peace.com/indexjour.htm.

22. Ibid.

communicate effectively with the extremist, left wing, radical secular progressives. We have two vastly different languages, and as Rudyard Kipling said, "*East is East and West is West and neither the twain shall meet*"![23] To paraphrase that saying to our current situation, "Middle East is Mid-East and West is West and neither the twain shall meet."

> *Dr. Michael Savage calls liberalism a mental disorder!*

Primary Targets of Terrorism and Urban Guerrilla Warfare

Primary Targets. The primary targets of terrorism include the following large gatherings of noncombatants (i.e., innocent civilians) anywhere including urban, suburban, or rural settings:

- Stadiums with football bowl games, baseball World Series games, and Olympic Games
- Major amusement parks and centers
- Train and bus stations
- Airports
- Airplanes
- Ships and commercial ocean liners
- Major hotels
- Restaurants
- Department stores
- Shopping centers and malls
- Churches
- Universities, colleges, and schools

Specific Primary Targets. The specific, primary targets of terrorists will include Hollywood and Beverly Hills (to get the Hollywood elite or the Hollywood mafia), houses of ill repute, homosexual social establishments, bath

---

23.   Rudyard Kipling (1865—1936), British writer, poet. "The Ballad of East and West," *Barrack-Room Ballads* (1892).

houses, massage parlors, nudist colony camps, X-rated movie theaters, beer breweries, prisons (to get the child molesters, rapists, and sodomists), and other places of ill-repute that the Isfasts despise.

Primary Targets of Urban Guerrilla Warfare. The primary targets of urban guerrilla warfare include any high-value target (both people and property) within large urban centers that have military fighting significance:

- Military bases and other installations
- Major aerospace and defense plants
- Ammunition manufacturing plants and depots
- Weapons factories
- Major NASA centers
- Major civilian R&D centers
- Seaports
- Planes
- International airports
- Radio and television stations
- Power generating plants
- Nuclear power plants
- Electrical substations
- Power grids
- Water tanks
- Aqueducts
- Train and bus stations
- Railroads
- Major highways and freeways
- Industrial complexes
- Bridges
- Tunnels
- Dams
- Gas storage facilities and petroleum storage depots
- Banks

- Newspaper plants
- Hospitals
- The military academies
- US embassies
- Beer breweries
- Sewage treatment plants

Specific Primary Targets of Urban Guerrilla Warfare. The specific, primary targets of terrorists in urban guerilla warfare will include the following:
- The White House
- The Capitol Building
- US Senate
- US House of Representatives
- Pentagon Building
- FBI Headquarters
- CIA Headquarters
- NSA Headquarters
- NASA Headquarters
- Peterson Air Force Base, Colorado (where the functions of the Cheyenne Mountain Operations Center were moved)
- Top 10 major cities in the US including:
  - New York City, NY
  - Los Angeles, CA
  - Chicago, IL
  - Houston, TX
  - Philadelphia, PA
  - Phoenix, AZ
  - San Antonio, TX
  - San Diego, CA
  - Dallas, TX
  - San Jose, CA

- Wall Street in Manhattan, NY
- Las Vegas, NV
- Fort Knox, KY
- Hollywood, CA
- Beverly Hills, CA
- Tall buildings, e.g., Empire State Building, Seattle Space Needle, Transamerica Building, Sears Building, and Chrysler Building
- Alaskan Pipeline
- Silicon Valley

Weak on Defense

The extreme, left wing, radical secular progressives (SPs) think the Isfasts will give them some slack when they meet face to face. However, these SPs will be surprised to find that they are the ones that the terrorists will behead first because the Isfasts despise everything that they are doing in the US and the world. Furthermore, since the SPs are "weak on defense" cowards, the Isfasts want them to win in the next elections so that they will be an easier target to overcome and conquer than would be the conservatives.

Congress Needs Major Overhaul

Vote Out All Incumbent Congress People. A bunch of losers, liars, thieves, cheats, and jackals fill the United States Senate. This is why President Theodore Roosevelt said, "*When you call roll in the Senate, the Senators do not know whether to answer 'present' or 'not guilty.'*" Furthermore, Mark Twain said, "*There is no distinctly Native American criminal class ... save Congress.*" *The Senate, like the House, needs a major overhaul.* We need to vote out all of the incumbent congress people and replace them with new blood. Then, it will take a few years before this new blood also turns into leukemia blood. After that, we will need to go through another blood transfusion. Edward Langley, artist (1928-95), said, "*What this country needs are more unemployed politicians.*" What wise words from a wise man.

> *The Senate, like the House, needs a major overhaul.*

We Only Have Political Hacks. *Not a single statesman exists either in the Congress or in politics.* We only have political hacks (e.g., Bill Clinton, Jimmy Carter, Ted Kennedy, John Kerry, Howard Dean, Jack Murtha, Nancy Pelosi, Hillary Clinton, Al Gore, Harry Reid, Al Sharpton, Chuck Schumer, Charlie Rangel, and other such wacky whackos), but no statesmen. Whatever happened to statesmen of the caliber of Teddy Roosevelt, Franklin D. Roosevelt, Harry Truman, Dwight D. Eisenhower, and Ronald Reagan?

> *Not a single statesman exists either in the Congress or in politics.*

Quality of Politicians at All-time Low. All we now have are a bunch of godless gigolos, liars, thieves, cheaters, pedophiles, and traitors running our country. *The quality of our politicians has plummeted to an all-time low ... even below used-car salesmen!* All they pursue include money, power, fame, women, and underage pages or very young congressional aides. Will Rogers said, "*I don't make jokes. I just watch the government and report the facts.*" As down as I am on politicians and politics, President Ronald Reagan gave them some hope when he said, "*Politics is not a bad profession. If you succeed, there are many rewards; if you disgrace yourself, you can always write a book.*"[24] After all, they are all doing it.

> *The quality of our politicians has plummeted to an all-time low ... even below used-car salesmen!*

Means of Terror

Besides the traditional weapons, terrorists will use the following means once they acquire the weapons, capability, and or opportunity:

- *Weapons of Mass Destruction (WMDs)*—Nuclear, Biological, and Chemical (NBC) or Chemical, Biological, and Radiological (CBR)

  o Nuclear Warfare (NW)—nuclear bombs and/or weapons including suitcase nuclear weapons

  o Biological Warfare (BW)—rapid spreading, deadly diseases, spores, and germs. This is also called germ warfare.

---

24. "Ronald Reagan's Wisdom," extracted on 9/27/06 from the following URL: http://www.newsmax.com, Riviera Beach: Florida, 2006.

- o Chemical Warfare (CW)—deadly poisonous gases, sprays, liquids, and gels

- o Radiological Warfare (RW)—"dirty bombs" using nuclear waste material for its enduring radiation effects

- **Cyber Warfare**—destruction or theft of data, databases, and data transmission using viruses, worms, Trojan horses, and other electronic means

- **Enhanced Effects Warfare (EEW)**—violence producing extraordinary effects by conventional means such as:

  - o Flying airplanes into skyscrapers

  - o Assassinations of political leaders

  - o Hijackings

  - o Skyjackings

  - o Mass casualties

Rules of Engagement

In real asymmetrical warfare, there is no such thing as rules of engagement. Asymmetrical warfare is "free-for-all" warfare. Islamo-fascist terrorists are unhampered by morals, ethics, and legalities. Islamo-fascists are amoral. If we are to prevail against them, we must do likewise. *We must be unshackled and unhampered by conventional warfare rules of engagement.* To triumph over the Isfasts, we must use every possible unconventional warfare strategy, tactic, means, technology, weaponry, tools, techniques, and methods.

Only Language Islamo-fascists Understand

Cast Off Political Correctness. The only language that Isfasts understand pertains to words such as force, power, kill, control, decapitate, humiliate, and pain. Hence, we should apply everything within our power and means to use these tools on them. When we inflict these tools on them, they under-

> *We must be unshackled and unhampered by conventional warfare rules of engagement.*

stand when we have the upper hand. When we apply the "political correctness" tools on them, they see us as weak. Hence, they become emboldened to keep pursuing their main goal in life, which is to achieve world domination and their idea of utopia. Noni Darwish said, "*We are strangling ourselves with our political correctness.*"[25]

> *We are strangling ourselves with our political correctness.*
>
> **Noni Darwish**

Fight Fire with Fire. We should use the language they understand. The only language the Isfasts understand is what they do. We need to do the same things that they do. If they kill, we need to kill. If they bomb us, we need to bomb them. *We must fight fire with fire.* Let us not kid ourselves. They are out to eradicate democracy, freedom, liberty, and the free-enterprise system. It is them or us. It is better to be them.

Isfasts Do Not Believe in Compromise

Because of the intolerance displayed by the Isfasts toward the West as well as the ultimate goal of the Isfasts (i.e., world domination), we have a problem that cannot be resolved through debate, discussion, diplomacy, or compromise. *The Isfasts do not believe in compromise.* It is all their way or the highway for us. It is impossible for diplomacy to work with such an unbendable position held by the Isfasts.

> *We must fight fire with fire.*

No Negotiating with Islamo-fascists

Never negotiate with terrorists. If they kill a hostage, we go after them with vengeance and wipe them off the map without delay. Teach them lessons they will never forget. That is the only language they understand. Send

> *Never negotiate with terrorists.*

---

25.   Darwish, Noni. Quote extracted from the television documentary titled "Obsession: The Threat of Radical Islam" shown on Fox News Television as hosted by E.D. Hill on November 25, 2006.

them to their twisted concept of heaven where they will live with 72 virgins. I am sorry, but that belief will never come to pass.

Ben Franklin may have said, "*They that can give up essential liberty to obtain a little temporary safety deserve neither liberty nor safety, and ultimately will have neither.*" I paraphrase that a little bit as follows: "*Secular progressives who will negotiate essential liberty to terrorists to obtain a little temporary safety deserve neither liberty nor safety and ultimately will have neither.*" Additionally, the terrorists will lop off their heads and roll those heads in the streets.

No Appeasement

You cannot appease our modern-day enemy. In negotiations, if you give them an inch, they will want a foot. If you give them a foot, they will want a mile. It will never end because their overall goal is world domination. Since we cannot appease them, then we must snuff them out. We must eradicate them from the face of the earth. We must eliminate them before they eliminate us. Do to terrorists as they would do to you … and then some.

> *You cannot appease our modern-day enemy.*

The cowardice policy of appeasement does not work and will never work. Discard it.

20 for 1

The Isfasts do not understand the New Testament principle of "Do unto others as you would have them do unto you." They only understand and apply the Old Testament principle of "*Eye for an eye; tooth for a tooth.*" Therefore, if that is all they understand, then that is what needs to be applied to them. *They kill 1 of us; we kill 10 of them. Better yet, we kill 20 of them for every 1 of us they kill.* That would make a greater impact on their twisted psyche.

> *They kill 1 of us; we kill 10 of them. Better yet, we kill 20 of them for every 1 of us they kill.*

Kill or Be Killed?

It is either kill or be killed. If given that choice, I would rather kill first than be killed first. Wouldn't you? General George S. Patton said, "*May God have mercy upon my enemies because I won't.*" We must do as General Patton said, "*We as attackers have the initiative; we must retain this tremendous advantage by always attacking rapidly, ruthlessly, viciously, and without rest.*" If we want to survive, that is what we must do! We must listen to the good general's words and put it into practice. I am sure that General Patton had read Sun Tzu. Sun Tzu said, "*Therefore, the good fighter will be terrible in his onset, and prompt in his decision.*"

Geneva Convention is Obsolete

Laboring under the viscous fluid called the Geneva Convention, we cannot effectively fight an enemy who:

- Wants to convert you to his religion or kill you by sawing off your head at the neck if you will not convert.

- Wants to dominate the world. World domination is their ultimate goal.

- Are psychopaths.

- Will gladly die as a suicide bomber to receive 72 virgins upon going to his twisted idea of heaven.

- Will wantonly kill innocent, non-military men, women, children, young/old/infirm people, innocent civilians, and anyone else for the sake of instilling terror in their minds.

- Uses coercion, pain, force, fear, intimidation, and terror tactics to get their way.

- Totally ignores the Geneva Convention.

Abandon the Geneva Convention

To win the war against Isfasts, we must abandon the Geneva Convention:

- Because it is obsolete when fighting in asymmetrical or asynchronous warfare

- If the enemy does not adhere to the Geneva Convention

> *To win the war against Isfasts, we must abandon the Geneva Convention.*

- Particularly when we arrive at the point of being in a final war for survival

What's Good for the Goose is Good for the Gander

All Bets are Off! If the terrorists (i.e., al-Qaida, Hezbollah, Hamas, Taliban, and other Isfasts) will bomb and wantonly kill innocent civilian men, women, children, the aged, the infirm, reporters, UN personnel, and Red Cross personnel, then all of their similar people are fair game for us. "*The sword without, and terror within, shall destroy both the young man and the virgin, the suckling also with the man of gray hairs.*" (Deut. 32:25)[26] All bets are off! *What's good for the goose is good for the gander.* Thus,

> **What's good for the goose is good for the gander.**

we will let the world know that we will not fight with one hand tied behind our backs any longer. *We shall fight ruthlessness with ruthlessness.* We shall fight fire with fire … only two orders of magnitude more.

A Tit-for-Tat War. If the terrorists will not adhere to any rules of engagement, then we too will not adhere to any rules of engagement. If the terrorists do not recognize and adhere to the tenets of the Geneva Convention, then we are not bound by the tenets of the Geneva Convention. We will fight a tit-for-tat war. Whatever the terrorists dish out, we will dish back to them an order-of-magnitude greater (even two

> **We shall fight ruthlessness with ruthlessness.**

orders of magnitude greater) retaliatory force and firepower. As General George S. Patton said, "*We won't just shoot the bastards, but rip out their living guts and use them to grease the treads of our tanks.*" Where is General Patton when we need him?

Retaliate Tit for Tat

No Such Thing as Collateral Damage. If the Isfasts poison our water supplies, we poison their water supplies. If the Isfasts use germ warfare (anthrax or whatever) on our people, we use germ warfare on their people. If the Isfasts

---

26. Deuteronomy 32:25, *The Holy Bible*.

use poison gas, we use poison gas. If the Isfasts blow up our power stations, we retaliate by blowing up their entire infrastructure of power stations, utilities, dams, bridges, highways, farms, airports, military bases, government buildings, and other infrastructure. *Forget about collateral damage! There is no such thing as collateral damage when we are fighting for our survival.*

We will Speak Their Language. If the Isfasts explode briefcase nuclear weapons in our big cities, we retaliate with nuke weapons and decimate their cities. We turn their cities into huge glass bowls, which would make nice lakes in the Middle Eastern deserts when filled with water. Also, blow out the Isfasts from their caves in the Afghan mountains by using tactical nuke weapons. If the Isfasts derail our trains and blow up our gasoline storage tanks, tanker trucks, and gas stations, we do likewise to them only an order-of-mag-

> *Forget about collateral damage! There is no such thing as collateral damage when we are fighting for our survival.*

nitude greater damage. If the Isfasts create havoc on our computers with viruses, worms, and Trojan horses, we do likewise to their systems. That's the language they understand. We will speak their language but only more so.

War is Not a Game

War is not a game. Hence, there is no such thing as "fair play" in war. There is no fairness. There is no "time out." There are no referees or umpires. You never go into the penalty box. In war, you destroy. You kill. You injure. You maim. You disable. You crush. You annihilate. You wipe out.

> *War is not a game.*

Those are the rules of the game (if you want to call it a game). Therefore, the Pendleton 8 did nothing wrong as we fight a war against Isfasts.

Moreover, remember this: General George S. Patton said, "*You're never beaten until you admit it.*" We will never lose because we will never admit it ... even if we must fight until the very last man is standing (unless, of course, the very last man is a secular progressive; then, all bets are off). We will never be placed into bondage by the Isfasts. Never, never, never! Karl von Clausewitz said, "*There is only one decisive victory: the last.*"[27] General Patton said, "*There's only one proper way for a professional soldier to die … the last bullet of the last battle of the last war.*"

No Such Thing as Fair Play in War

In all-out war, we should never stifle or curtail ourselves by playing fair. We should only play to win. As the famed Green Bay Packers Football Coach and General Manager Vince Lombardi said, "*Winning isn't everything; it's the only thing.*" In war, winning is the only thing because, if you lose, you are either slaughtered, or you will forever live in bondage. That is the only alternative to winning. Bondage is no

> ### *Winning isn't everything; it's the only thing.*
>
> **Coach Vince Lombardi, Green Bay Packers**

way to live. Remember, Ronald Reagan said, "*It is better to be dead than red.*" Yes, it is better to be mud than a radical Muslim. It is better to be free than a radical Islamite. Even their own members (particularly women) do not enjoy the freedoms that we Americans enjoy.

Collateral Damage?

There should be no such thing as "collateral damage" in asynchronous or asymmetrical warfare. Did we think about collateral damage when we bombed German cities ending World War II in Europe? Did we think about collateral damage when we dropped atomic bombs on Hiroshima and Nagasaki in Japan ending World War II in the Pacific? Did we think about collateral damage when we napalmed the Vietcong in Vietnam and when we spread "agent orange" throughout the Vietnam jungles? No! Agent Orange negatively affected even our own war fighters as well as the enemy fighters. It was fratricide! *Collateral damage should not hamper us in all-out war.*

---

27. Karl von Clausewitz, "Clausewitz Quotations." Extracted on 12/10/06 from the following URL: http://www.military-quotes.com/Clausewitz.htm.

Fog of War

Yes, the United States killed hundreds of civilians (maybe even thousands) in Afghanistan through "collateral damage" bombings. We also bombed and killed around

> *Collateral damage should not hamper us in all-out war.*

60 of the Afghan warlords from one faction in a convoy traveling to Hamid Karzai's inauguration because a competing faction told the US Navy that the Taliban leaders were in that convoy. It was an error for which the United States apologized. These kinds of errors fall under the "fog of war" mistakes. That is why it is important to verify intelligence from one warlord's words. However, if we do not recognize collateral damage as suggested above, this political correctness approach should be no more.

Fratricide

In warfare, fratricide is the unintentional killing of our own, coalition, or allied forces. *Fratricide occurs because of stupidity, lack of knowing the difference between friend or foe, and proper identification of the good guys versus the bad guys.* We need better identification friend or foe (IFF) capabilities and systems. It seems, sometimes, that we kill more of our own than the enemy ever kills. What is wrong with that picture anyway?

> *Fratricide occurs because of stupidity, lack of knowing the difference between friend or foe, and proper identification of the good guys versus the bad guys.*

Palestinian-Israeli Conflict

Ingredients for Peace. Peace will prevail between the Palestinians and Israelis only when the following "six points" occur:

1. The Israelis and Palestinians show mutual respect for each other and practice the principle of "live and let live."

2. The Palestinians and Israelis adopt and believe in the basic human right of "freedom of religion."

3. The Israelis and Palestinians practice their own religions, which espouse "love and charity" towards all.

4. The Palestinians and Israelis allow Christianity to be embraced among those of their people who desire it.

5. The Israelis and Palestinians intermarry.

6. The Palestinians and Israelis live among each other as good neighbors.

Masters of Their Own Destinies. If the Israelis and Palestinians desire to continue killing off each other, then, they will continue to embrace and perpetuate hatred, anger, prejudice, bias, revenge, racism, jealousy, fear, greed, and everything that is undesirable to good, God-fearing people. They both have a choice. They have their free agency. They will bear the consequences of whatever they choose. It is a very sad situation in the Middle East.

> *One of the most asinine statements that I have ever heard is that "one man's terrorist is another man's freedom fighter."*

Mutual Definition Required. One problem of the Israelis and Palestinians is that they have no mutually agreed upon definition of "terrorism." *One of the most asinine statements that I have ever heard is that "one man's terrorist is another man's freedom fighter."* That makes no sense when we define "terrorism" as the intentional targeting and killing of innocent civilians (i.e., noncombatants) using suicide bombers to wreak fear and havoc in the lives of all people in Israel.

Intention is the Key. The intent is an important differentiator here. Yes, the Israelis are killing more Palestinian civilians than Palestinian combatants. However, it is because the Hamas combatants hide among the civilians and, hence, collateral damage kills the civilians. The Israeli combatants do not intentionally target and kill the innocent Palestinian civilians. However, on the other hand, *it is the prime intent of the Palestinian suicide bombers to kill innocent civilians* (both Israelis and Palestinians) for the purpose of wreaking fear and havoc in the hearts and minds of all peoples in Israel (and the world for that matter).

Yasser Arafat the Terrorist. Before the dastardly terrorist Yasser Arafat passed on to inherit his 72 virgins, his terrorists went after innocent Israeli civilians as their primary target. He killed hundreds, indeed thousands, of Israeli citizens using human suicide bombers. To think that the Nobel organization jointly awarded the 1994 Nobel Peace Prize to that little, sniveling terrorist just made a mockery of Mr. Alfred Nobel and his Nobel Peace Prize program. Disgusting!

> *It is the prime intent of the Palestinian suicide bombers to kill innocent civilians....*

Human Shields Used. On the other hand, Ariel Sharon's military force targets those terrorists who kill innocent Israeli civilians as well as the Palestinian police (who, basically, are a *paramilitary* force). "Collateral effects" kill innocent civilians because those Palestinian terrorists (Hamas) cowardly shield themselves among innocent Palestinian civilians. When bombs or rockets kill the Hamas terrorists, unfortunately, they also kill the innocent civilian shields. Saddam Hussein employed a similar barbaric tactic during the Gulf Wars.

Paramilitary Groups. In the paragraph above, *paramilitary*, like *paramedic* and *paralegal*, comes from Greek *para* ("beside"). *Paramilitary* means auxiliary military, that is, something not quite military performing military duties. There are political connotations to "paramilitary," which often override the original meaning. Those political connotations, however, are localized and contradictory. There are paramilitary units that are an official legislated arm of the government, anti-government armed units that claim military status, civilian paramilitary units that are neither, and other groups that are something in between.[28]

Boils Down to Intent. *The core of the Israeli-Palestinian problem boils down to intent.* Is it the intent of the Palestinians to eradicate totally the Israelis from that area of the world? If the answer is "yes," then no peace is possible, and the Israelis then need to eradicate the Palestinians in order to survive. If "no," then they (both the Palestinians and Israelis) need to get to the peace table and work out a lasting agreement. That's it! It is a very simple yet complicated solution.

---

28.   Extracted on 9/12/06 from Wikipedia, the free encyclopedia, at URL: http://en.wikipedia.org/wiki/Paramilitary.

Pakistan-India Conflict

Working Together is Key. Both India and Pakistan should stop fighting each other and start working together to eradicate terrorism in both of their countries. They should capture terrorists on their homeland and turn them over to the other country for trial and disposal. India should turn over the terrorists captured in their country to Pakistan for trial and punishment. Pakistan should turn over the terrorists captured in their country to India for trial and punishment. How each country deals with the terrorists turned over to them will truly indicate their feelings toward terrorists and terrorism.

> *The core of the Israeli-Palestinian problem boils down to intent.*

Terrorists are Evil People. Discard the statement that *"one man's terrorist is another man's freedom fighter."* A terrorist is not a freedom fighter, period. *A terrorist does not fight for freedom.* The terrorists fight to eradicate the "so-called infidels," civilians, Christians, Americans, democratic and freedom loving peoples, Westerners, and anyone who do not hold to their religious and political beliefs. *Terrorists fight to put all unbelievers in bondage. Terrorism represents the face of evil. Hence, terrorists are evil people whom we must destroy.*

> *A terrorist does not fight for freedom.*

Agreement in Terminology Needed. An Isfast terrorist is a person who meets one or both of these following conditions:

- Terrorists do not wear a bona fide military uniform of any country with the accepted insignia on the uniform

- Terrorists kill innocent civilian victims (including

> *Terrorists fight to put all unbelievers in bondage. Terrorism represents the face of evil. Hence, terrorists are evil people whom we must destroy.*

men, women, children, old folks, and the sick and afflicted) because they hate them. They do this mass killing:

  o By any means possible for the shock effect/impact

o   To make a political statement

o   To put fear/terror in the hearts and minds of the general population

If both countries will agree to these principles, they will be on their way to resolving their mutual conflict and will start living in peace. It all must start with mutual cooperation.

The 10-Point Plan to End the War on Terrorism

The Solution is Available. Someone once asked the question: "Does anyone have a solution to end the War on Terrorism?" I said I did and gave the following "10-Point Plan" to win the War on Terrorism:

1. *Declare War Officially.* Get Congress to declare war officially on al-Qaida. A resolution or proclamation is not enough. We must have a declaration of war. That way, it clearly defines the traitors.

2. *Generals to Fight the War.* Leave fighting the War on Terrorism to military generals.

3. *One Goal: To Win at All Cost.* Give the generals the mandate to "win the war" *by whatever means necessary.* After all, "war is hell."

4. *Keep Politicians Out.* Politicians—stay out of running the war. If they want to be involved, put them in uniform and place them on the front lines of our offense.

5. *Discard Geneva Convention.* The Geneva Convention does not apply to terrorists … only to uniformed soldiers of a bona fide nation. Terrorists do not come under the protection of the Geneva Convention. There are no applicable rules of engagement to protect them. After all, they are animals/insects that we need to exterminate.

> *Give the generals the mandate to "win the war" by whatever means necessary.*

6. ***Bring Traitors to Trial.*** Bring to trial those sorry, disloyal Americans who display treasonous behavior. Execute them. *Where is Joseph McCarthy when we need him?*

> # Where is Joseph McCarthy when we need him?

7. ***Level Terrorist Rat Holes with Tactical Nukes.*** In war, whenever a city is infested with the terrorists, drop 100 each "bunker busters" to level the city to rubble. Apply the scorched-earth doctrine. If it becomes necessary to get to deeply buried bunkers and underground command centers, create a glass crater with tactical nuclear weapons. General George S. Patton said, "*Use the means at hand to inflict the maximum amount of wound, death, and destruction on the enemy in the minimum amount of time.*" Tactical nukes will neatly fill this bill.

8. ***Use Enemy Uniform.*** Dress our war-fighters in the same uniforms (including *jilbab, hijab, thobes,* and prayer sets for men, women, and children) worn by the terrorists and get them to infiltrate the population to ferret out terrorists. Recruit loyal Arab Americans, Muslim Americans, and Islamic Americans as our war-fighters so that they can blend in with the crowd.

> # Tactical nukes will neatly fill this bill.

   a. In modern day usage, jilbāb refers to a long, flowing, baggy overgarment worn by some Muslim women. They believe that this fulfills the Islamic demands for modesty, or hijab. The modern jilbāb covers the entire body, except for hands, feet, face, and head. A scarf or wrap covers the head. Some women will also cover the hands, feet, and face. In Indonesia, the word jilbab is used for a headscarf rather than a long baggy overgarment (Geertz).[29]

   b. Hijab or hijāb is the Arabic term for "barrier." In some Arabic-speaking countries and Western countries, the word hijab primarily refers to a headscarf worn by Muslim women. However, in Islamic scholarship, hijab usually takes on the wider meaning of dressing in a way

---

29. Extracted on 9/11/06 from Wikipedia, the free encyclopedia, at the following URL: http://en.wikipedia.org/wiki/JilbÄb. Quoted from Clifford Geertz—*Available Light: Anthropological Reflections on Philosophical Topics*, Princeton University Press, 2000.

that covers the hair, arms, and feet. The word used in the Quran for a headscarf or veil is *khimar*.[30]

c. The thobe is perfectly suited for the hot desert climate of Saudi Arabia. The Quran states that a man should be judged by his deeds not on his appearance so the thobe also expresses equality. The thobe is a loose, long-sleeved, ankle-length garment. Summer thobes are white and made of cotton, and winter thobes can be darker and made of wool.[31]

9. ***Apply Martial Law.*** Declare and maintain Martial Law throughout cities and regions in Afghanistan and Iraq with high insurgent density until all insurgents are liquidated. The *American Heritage® Dictionary* defines "martial law" as temporary rule by military authorities, imposed on a civilian population especially in time of war or when civil authority has broken down; the law imposed on an occupied territory by occupying military forces. *If the current Afghanistan and Iraqi governments oppose this measure, then pull out our troops, bring them home, and let the current governments fight the war themselves. That should quickly bring them to their senses.*

> **If the current Afghanistan and Iraqi governments oppose this measure, then pull out our troops, bring them home, and let the current governments fight the war themselves. That should quickly bring them to their senses.**

10. ***Fight Fire with Fire.*** Use exactly the same tactics and strategies that terrorists use. *Fight fire with fire.* That is the only language they understand. For example, consider using:

> **Fight fire with fire.**

---

30.   Extracted on 9/11/06 from Wikipedia, the free encyclopedia, at the following URL: http://en.wikipedia.org/wiki/Hijab.

31.   Extracted on 9/11/06 from The Saudi Arabian Thobe website, which can be found at the following URL: http://www.toursaudiarabia.com/thobe.html.

a. Civilian clothing as uniforms for our war fighters

b. Human shields

c. Human suicide bombers

d. Improvised explosive devices (IEDs)

e. Roadside bombs and mines

f. Filmed decapitations with dull blades and provide videos to al-Jazeera and CNN

g. Indiscriminate bombing of all enemy populations

h. Dissemination of disinformation

i. Use booby traps

j. Kidnap *imams* and use them as bargaining chips

k. Blow up Muslim mosques that are suspected of serving as Isfast sanctuaries and harboring terrorists and weapons caches

l. Kill family members of Isfast leaders. It worked well against Muammar Abu Minyar al-Qaddafi (pronounced Gaddafi) of Libya.

We Need General George Patton. There it is ... The 10-point Plan to end all hostilities caused by Isfast terrorists in war zones. There shall be no more pussyfooting around with traitorous pinheads. *Where is General George S. Patton, Jr., when we really need him?* We need a military leader who loves war as Patton did. He said,

> **Where is General George S. Patton, Jr., when we really need him?**

"*Magnificent! Compared to war, all other forms of human endeavor shrink to insignificance. God help me, I do love it so!*" Patton further said, "*No bastard ever won a war by dying for his country. He won it by making the other poor dumb bastard die for his country.*" So, let us get those Isfast terrorist cockroaches to die for their own twisted cause and earn themselves 72 virgins each in their distorted view of heaven.

General Vernon Chong Understands. Dr. Vernon Chong, Major General, United States Air Force (USAF), Retired, said, *"The Muslims fully know what is riding on this war, and therefore are completely committed to winning, at any cost. We better know it too and likewise be committed to winning at any cost. Why do I go on at such lengths about the results of losing? Simple. Until we recognize the costs of losing, we cannot unite and really put 100 percent of our thoughts and efforts into winning. And it is going to take that 100 percent effort to win."*[32]

> *Until we recognize the costs of losing, we cannot unite and really put 100 percent of our thoughts and efforts into winning. And it is going to take that 100 percent effort to win.*
>
> **Dr. Vernon Chong,**
> **Major General, USAF, Retired**

---

32.   Vernon Chong, "Muslims, Terrorists, and the USA: A Different Spin on the Iraq War." Dr. Chong is a retired Air Force surgeon and past commander of Wilford Hall Medical Center in San Antonio, Texas (retired on November 1, 1994). For his bio, go to http://www.af.mil/bios/alpha.asp?alpha=C.

Chapter 5

Military Strategies to Counter Isfasts

The *American Heritage® Dictionary* defines "strategy" as the science and art of using all the forces of a nation to execute approved plans as effectively as possible during peace or war; a plan of action resulting from strategy or intended to accomplish a specific goal; the art or skill of using stratagems in endeavors such as politics and business. Sun Tzu said, *"All men can see the tactics whereby I conquer, but what none can see is the strategy out of which victory is evolved."*[33]

All of the following military strategies are available (no holds barred) for employment. One of the most skilled Japanese swordsmen in history, Miyamoto Musashi, said, *"Strategy is the craft of the warrior."*[34] He further said, *"Someone once said 'Immature strategy is the cause of grief.' That was a true saying."*[35]

> ### The best form of defense is attack.
> #### General Karl von Clausewitz

First-Strike Strategy

"First strike" is a viable and effective strategy. The best defense is a good offense. Karl von Clausewitz, Prussian general and military strategist, said, *"The best form of defense is attack."*[36] General George S. Patton said, *"In case of doubt, attack."* Miyamoto Musashi said, *"Because you can win quickly by taking the lead, it is one of the most important things in strategy."*[37]

---

33. Sun Tzu, *The Art of War*. Extracted on 10/15/06 from The Internet Classics Archive of the Massachusetts Institute of Technology at URL: http://classics.mit.edu/Tzu/artwar.html.

34. Miyamoto Musashi, *A Book of Five Rings*, *"Go Rin No Sho."* Extracted on 10/13/06 from URL http://www.miyamotomusashi.com/gorin.htm.

35. Ibid.

36. Karl von Clausewitz, *On War*. Extracted on 12/10/06 from the following URL: http://www.military-quotes.com/Clausewitz.htm.

37. Miyamoto Musashi, *A Book of Five Rings*, *"Go Rin No Sho."* Extracted on 10/13/06 from http://www.miyamotomusashi.com/gorin.htm.

Always Take the Offensive Strategy

Better to Attack Than to Be Attacked. *Always, always, always take the offensive over the defensive.* Defense works in winning football games, but does not work in winning all-out wars. In warfare, an offensive strategy works better than does a defensive strategy. I would rather attack than be attacked. Sun Tzu said, *"Security against defeat implies defensive tactics; ability to defeat the enemy means taking the offensive. Standing on the defensive indicates insufficient strength; attacking, a superabundance of strength."*[38]

Hunker-down Strategy. The hunker-down strategy did not work very well for Saddam Hussein in the first Gulf War when American bombs from B-52s nearly decimated his Republican Guard. President George H.W. Bush made the big mistake by not going all the way and conquering Iraq in the first go-around. Miyamoto Musashi said, *"Everything can collapse.*

> *Always, always, always take the offensive over the defensive.*

Houses, bodies, and enemies collapse when their rhythm becomes deranged. In large-scale strategy, when the enemy starts to collapse, you must pursue him without letting the chance go. If you fail to take advantage of your enemies' collapse, they may recover."[39] Moreover, that's exactly what Saddam Hussein did.

Prussian General Karl von Clausewitz said, *"If the enemy is to be coerced, you must put him in a situation that is even more unpleasant than the sacrifice you call on him to make. The hardships of the situation must not be merely transient—at least not in appearance. Otherwise, the enemy would not give in, but would wait for things to improve."*[40] Do not let the enemy rest and recover to fight another day. Pursue him and kill him so that he cannot come back at you in the future.

Remember, General George S. Patton, said, *"In war the only sure defense is offense, and the efficiency of the offense depends on the warlike souls of those conduct-*

38.   Sun Tzu, *The Art of War.* Extracted on 10/15/06 from The Internet Classics Archive of the Massachusetts Institute of Technology at the following URL: http://classics.mit.edu/Tzu/artwar.html.

39.   Miyamoto Musashi, *A Book of Five Rings*, *"Go Rin No Sho."* Extracted on 10/13/06 from http://www.miyamotomusashi.com/gorin.htm.

40.   Karl von Clausewitz, Clausewitz Quotations. Extracted on 12/10/06 from URL http://www.military-quotes.com/Clausewitz.htm.

ing it." Further, General Patton said, "*Always take the offensive … never dig in.*" Furthermore, he said, "*Fixed fortifications are monuments to the stupidity of man.*" Therefore, always be on the prowl. We should avoid decimation by not being sitting ducks.

Overwhelming Force Strategy

Do not pussyfoot around. When you attack, hit the enemy with your best shots. Knock them on their rear ends with the first barrage of firepower. As a winning boxer uses a flurry of deadly jabs, we should do likewise in battle. Do whatever it takes to win the fight. President Teddy Roosevelt said, "*The unforgivable crime is soft hitting. Do not hit at all if it can be avoided; but never hit softly.*" President Ronald Reagan said, "*Of the four wars in my lifetime, none came about because the US was too strong.*"[41]

> *Use tactical nuclear weapons (TNWs) in warfare.*

Tactical Nuclear Warfare Strategy

Use tactical nuclear weapons (TNWs) in warfare. Using tactical nukes would end wars quickly. We must extinguish the enemy's will to win and the will to fight. Once we do that, the war is over.

I liken Miyamoto Musashi's **long sword** to **TNWs**. He said, "*To master the virtue of the long sword is to govern the world and oneself, thus the long sword is the basis of strategy. The principle is 'strategy by means of the long sword.' If he attains the virtue of the long sword, 1 man can beat 10 men. Just as 1 man can beat 10, so a 100 men can beat 1,000 [men], and 1,000*

> *With a single explosion, one pilot using a TNW can kill 10,000 terrorists and terrorist sympathizers.*

---

41. "Ronald Reagan's Wisdom," extracted on 9/27/06 from http://www.newsmax.com, Riviera Beach: Florida, 2006.

can beat 10,000. In my strategy, 1 man is the same as 10,000, so this strategy is the complete warrior's craft."[42]

Hence, *with a single explosion, one pilot using a TNW can kill 10,000 terrorists and terrorist sympathizers.* The best time to hit them is when they hold a huge anti-American rally in their capital's town square (like Red Square, for example). One TNW can eliminate 100,000 to 1,000,000 people in one fell swoop. What a strategy!

Dirty Nukes Strategy

Use "dirty nuclear" weapons. If we do not use it first, the Isfasts will be using it soon. Then, as usual, we will be playing a catch-up ballgame. Some day, their first strike may render us incapable of catching up. Always stay in the driver's seat by taking the offensive and using your strongest weapons first.

Shock-and-Awe Strategy

Shock and awe the enemy with overwhelming offensive force. I am not talking about the joke of a "shock and awe" as demonstrated in Baghdad during the second Gulf War or the War with Iraq. I refer to a real, honest-to-goodness "shock and awe" using tactical nuke weapons. Surprise and shock always give you the upper hand over any enemy.

> *Surprise and shock always give you the upper hand over any enemy.*

Assassination Strategy

Assassinate Axis of Evil leaders and key terror leaders using hired, professional assassins. Some people would do anything for money. However, John Wilkes Booth and Lee Harvey Oswald did it without remuneration when they assassinated President Abraham Lincoln and President John F. Kennedy, respectively. Sirhan Sirhan, an Isfast terrorist, did it at no cost when he assassinated Bobby Kennedy.

---

42.   Miyamoto Musashi, *A Book of Five Rings*, *"Go Rin No Sho."* Extracted on 10/13/06 from http://www.miyamotomusashi.com/gorin.htm.

Regime Change Strategy

Target Iraq, North Korea, and Syria. *Eradicate governments that foster, harbor, finance, and train Isfast terrorists.* If the president is going to make such statements that we are coming after countries that support terrorism, then we should back up that strong rhetoric with action and actually do it. Hence, we should turn Iraq, North Korea, and Syria over to more civilized, humane rulers.

> *Eradicate governments that foster, harbor, finance, and train Isfast terrorists.*

A Good Defense is a Better Offense. Plans should be in place to effect such regime changes. These defensive strategies should not be unplanned events or on-the-spur-of-the-moment actions. Remember, we are not wantonly out to conquer other nations. We only strive to protect ourselves from those who outwardly profess to kill all of us in a nuclear attack. Hence, *a good defense is a better offense.*

> *A good defense is a better offense.*

Eliminate al-Qaida Strategy

Eliminate al-Qaida, which is Osama bin Laden's Isfast terrorist network base. Al-Qaida is the driving force behind all other Isfast organizations such as the Taliban, Hamas, and Hezbollah. First, cut off the head of the snake, i.e., get Osama bin Laden. Then, get the body of the snake by eradicating all of the al-Qaida terrorists. Finally, shut off the war resources to the Taliban, Hamas, and Hezbollah.

Remove the Cancer Strategy

Deal with Isfast terrorists as you would a cancer. You have to cut it out

> *George H. W. Bush's biggest mistake was to refrain from entering Baghdad and zapping Saddam Hussein on that first go-around.*

using surgery or poison it using radiation and/or chemotherapy. We should first isolate it and then kill it. General Colin Powell had it right during the first Gulf War. *George H.W. Bush's biggest mistake was to refrain from entering Baghdad and zapping Saddam Hussein on that first go-around.* Had he done that, we would have avoided the problems in Iraq that we are dealing with today.

Genocide Strategy

Exterminate Every Isfast Terrorist. Conduct genocide on all Isfast terrorists. "Genocide" is the systematic and planned extermination of an entire national, racial, political, or ethnic group. In this case, the Isfast terrorists comprise a political group. Exterminate every Isfast terrorist on the face of the earth.

Take No Prisoners. This is a worldwide war. We must kill them on the spot instead of bringing them to court or incarcerating them in the Guantanamo (or Gitmo for short) prison. *Do not capture any terrorist.* The only language they understand is death. Even then, they erroneously think they are going to dwell with Allah. Little do they know that they will go straight to Hades to live with the Son of the Morning, i.e., Satan? However, it will be more like "mourning" than "morning."

> *Do not capture any terrorist.*

Cut Off Resources and Supplies Strategy

Cut off the terrorist and Taliban forces financial resources and war-making capability. Choke them at points that will slow down their ability to fight. Cut off and destroy the terrorists' food and water supplies. Kill the terrorists' livestock to starve their population.

Destroy-from-Within Strategy

Get terrorists to mistrust and fight each other. Create internal strife. *Divide and conquer.* Destroy their morals and morale. As they attempt to destroy us from within (as aided by the cowardly SPs), we should do the same to them.

> *Divide and conquer.*

Moral Decay Strategy

American Decadence. Establish a long-term program to destroy the Isfast morals of their children. Get at their children. Tempt their children with what their parents would call "American decadence." First, have aircraft fly over enemy territory and drop candy on their cities for their children to pick up and eat. Then, airdrop care package using small parachutes. These care packages would include such things as junk food, sweets, comic books, paperback books, jeans, and other tame items.

Destroy from Within. As their children grow and start to crave for more American goods, send them rock and roll music, Coke and Pepsi, TV soap operas, and movies. Then, get them to enjoy hamburgers, bacon, pork, liquor, illicit sex, pornography, and drugs. Finally, get them to question and cast off their religion. In other words, *destroy them from within just as the SPs are destroying the United States from within.*

Surreptitious Campaign Strategy

Conduct a surreptitious campaign against all Isfast terrorists. "Surreptitious" means to obtain, do, or make by clandestine, secret, or stealthy means. Go after terrorists with a hidden force (using undercover men, paramilitary force, guerrillas, covert operations, snipers, assassins, silencers, sleepers, and moles) that quietly get terrorists sans publicity or fanfare. *Terrorists would disappear one by one. Then, one day, there will be none!*

> **Destroy them from within just as the SPs are destroying the United States from within.**

Unconventional Warfare Strategy

Conduct unconventional warfare against the Isfast terrorists. Use unconventional tactics, weapons, and uniforms. Use unconventional sources and methods of gathering surveillance data. Use unconventional platforms for transportation. Use unconventional tools, para-

> **Terrorists would disappear one by one. Then, one day, there will be none.**

phernalia, and means of rendering the enemy incapable of resisting and carrying on his world domination objectives.

Hit-and-Run Warfare Strategy

Conduct hit-and-run warfare on the Isfast terrorists. Conduct raids, *blitzkrieg* (lightning war), and stealth warfare on terrorist training camps and cells. Take the quick-strike option. Hit the nuclear development facilities of Iran and North Korea sooner rather than later.

Commando Raids/Missions Strategy

Super-Secret Organization. Establish a super-secret, dedicated organization to pursue and eliminate key terrorist leaders outside of the continental United States (OCONUS):

- Similar to Special Operations Forces (SOFs)
    - Special Forces (SF) "Green Berets"
    - Rangers
    - Special Operations Aviation
    - Psychological Operations (PSYOPs)
    - Civil Affairs (CA)
    - Signal and Support
    - SEALs (Navy Sea-Air-Land Forces) and special boat units
    - Delta Force, Air Force special operations squadrons
- WW II-type British Commandos
- Los Angeles Police Department (LAPD)-type Special Weapons and Tactics (SWAT) Teams
- "Dirty Dozen" movie approach where a US Army major was assigned a dozen convicted murderers to train and lead them into a mass assassination mission of German officers in World War II
- Whatever else you may want to call this super-secret organization

Commando-type Raids. Conduct commando-type raids and missions on Isfast leaders using secret SOF-type forces in small teams. Deploy crack US and

British commandos and elite fighters to perform covert operations, sabotage, and seek and destroy Isfast terrorist leaders. Parachute these strike forces into enemy territory at night. Have them accomplish their mission, and then bring them out by attack helicopters and tilt-rotor aircraft.

Cut off Snake's Head. Go after the head of the snake and cut it off. That is the best way to render the body incapable and useless. Every time a new head rises, cut it off … like we did with Abu Musab al-Zarqawi. He cut off enough heads, so we blasted him with a bomb. He is just as dead as those whom he beheaded. However, he had blood all over his hands and clothing when he beheaded his hostages. Nice guy. He is now dead. That's what counts.

Higher Authority Strategy

We must continue being a God-fearing nation. Our forefathers established our nation on "Christian" principles. Hence, we should pray to God for protection. The secular progressives (extremist, left wing, radical liberals) have moved our country away from God over the past half century. We must return to God if we expect to survive as a free nation. President Ronald Reagan said, *"If we ever forget that we're one nation under God, then we will be a nation gone under."*[43] The traitorous SPs are moving us closer and closer to a nation gone under.

> *The traitorous SPs are moving us closer and closer to a nation gone under.*

Scorched-Earth Policy Strategy

Drop millions of leaflets over cities (e.g., Faluga, Sunni or Sunni Triangle, and South Lebanon) telling innocent citizens to clear out of there within 48 hours. Then, after that time has elapsed, level those cities using the carpet-bombing approach. Apply the "scorched earth" strategy to warfare. [***Note:*** In the press, writers also spell "Faluga" as Falluga, Falugah, Fallugah, Faluja, Falujah, Falluja, and Fallujah. Go figure! It just proves that nobody really knows the correct spelling of that town's name.]

---

43.   "Ronald Reagan's Wisdom," extracted on 9/27/06 from http://www.newsmax.com, Riviera Beach: Florida, 2006.

OCONUS Guerrilla Warfare Strategy

Recruit AMIs for Guerrilla Warfare. Conduct OCONUS guerrilla warfare against Isfast countries (particularly in countries such as Iran, Syria, Lebanon, Egypt, Saudi Arabia, and Pakistan). Our guerrillas are members of an irregular, usually indigenous military unit operating in small bands to undermine the Isfasts throughout the world. Recruit good AMIs, those who detest the Isfasts and their war against civilization, to join the small bands that undermine the worldwide terrorist network.

Underground. Establish an underground force of AMIs freedom fighters (these will be true freedom fighters). Use their women, particularly those who are very disgruntled with the degrading way the Isfasts treat them. Women using the *burkas* make good disguises and cover for them while they do their good deeds.

Sleeper Agents. They use sleeper agents; we should also use sleeper agents in their countries. Recruit American AMIs to serve as sleeper agents in Afghanistan, Iraq, Libya, Iran, Egypt, Saudi Arabia, Sudan, and Pakistan. Send our sleeper agents to await missions in these countries. Have them move into new neighborhoods where residents do not know each other.

Terrorize Their Countries. Do what the terrorists do. Have our sleeper agents burrow deep into the local culture, leading normal AMI lives while awaiting orders. Get into their networks, cells, countries, government, and communities to conduct espionage, subversion, sabotage, covert operations, and guerrilla warfare. *Terrorize their countries.*

> *Terrorize their countries.*

Subversion. Overthrow, destroy, ruin, and/or undermine the terrorist network and harboring countries/governments by corrupting the character, morals, or allegiance of the leaders and members of the network or the leaders and people of the countries/governments.

Get Them on Their Home Turf. Track down an Isfast leader and his band of fellow terrorists on their home turf. Force them to go underground (literally). Then, apply the Groundhog Tactic (see chapter on Tactics) on them.

Search and Destroy. Use the search and destroy tactic. Never give up pursuing them. Overturn every

> *Be like a pit bull. Bite onto them and never let go until they are either in Gitmo or dead ... preferably dead.*

rock. Enter every cave and tunnel. Find them and zap them. Make them feel sorry that they had attacked us in our homeland.

Hot Pursuit. Focus and aggressively pursue these Isfasts as well as the nations that harbor them. *Be like a pit bull. Bite onto them and never let go until they are either in Gitmo or dead … preferably dead.* That is when you can consider the mission accomplished.

Insurgency. Use military insurgency tactics to create revolt, uprising, rebellion, or insurrection among the peoples of terrorist-harboring countries. Cause the people in Iran, Syria, North Korea, and other such countries to rise up against their currently established leaders.

Death-multiplier Approach. Kidnap Isfast soldiers and sympathizers. For every American soldier and/or civilian the enemy kidnaps and kills, we kill 20 Isfasts. Twenty for 1 should be our advertised motto. That is a fair measure of the value of their people. I am sure you have heard of "force multipliers." This is the "death-multiplier" approach.

Surgical Implants. When we capture a severely injured or wounded Isfast terrorist, keep him sedated and incoherent. Perform surgery on his injuries. Implant a miniature-transmitting device (like what is in the airplane's "black box"). Release the Isfast terrorist to his country after he recovers. Track him until he contacts and communicates with his Isfast leaders. Then, surgically pinpoint-bomb those leaders.

Terrorist Networks/Cells. Map out the terrorist networks and cells. Set up our own networks and cells to learn how they operate. *To fight them, emulate them.*

Undercover Agents. Use undercover CIA agents in this war on terrorism.

Water Supply. If the terrorists poison our water supply, poison the terrorists' water supplies. Only increase the concentration by 10 or 20-fold.

Bio-terrorism. If the terrorists conduct bio-terrorism on us, conduct it right back on them—only give them back much more than they dish out (10 times more; even 20 times more). Give more than we receive.

> *To fight them, emulate them.*

Women. Work on their women and accentuate all of the repressive injustices currently done to them by their own leaders. Get them to recognize and desire women's rights. Get them to desire suffrage, casting off their head cover, and getting an education. Get them to become professionals and work outside of the home. Get them to wear makeup, wear modern hairdos, and to use sex as a weapon. Get them to demand equal rights and equal pay for equal work. Get them to form organizations like the National Organization for Women (NOW). Disrupt the family structure and increase the divorce rate.

CONUS Paramilitary Force Strategy

Establishing the Force. Establish a paramilitary force under the Department of Homeland Security (DHS) within the United States to combat the Isfast cells. Call this force the United States Counterterrorist Force (USCF). Form this paramilitary force with professionally paid volunteers in every major city of the US and worldwide. The paramilitary forces will be well-trained civilian groups. They will be organized in military fashion to operate in place of or to assist regular military forces and local police departments.

Form Counter-Terror Cells. They will identify, track, capture, thwart, and kill Isfast terrorists in our CONUS cities and in major cities throughout the world. Establish our own cells in major cities throughout the US and the world. Operate these cells similar in manner to the Isfast terror cells. We must counter terrorism using the same strategies and tactics of the Isfast terrorists. In other words, *fight terror with terror.*

Qualifications and Objectives. This paramilitary force will be civilians dressed in civilian clothing, will carry weapons, and may be former military, FBI, CIA, border patrol, police, and other suitably trained personnel. Their primary goals are to:

> *Fight terror with terror.*

(1) Perform surveillance on Isfast terrorists
(2) Track/tail these terrorists
(3) Conduct raids to seek and destroy terrorists throughout the CONUS

They will be trained and able to communicate in Arabic, skilled in martial arts, and proficient at urban guerrilla warfare.

Focus on Counterterrorism. The difference between these civilian forces and the military and city police is that the paramilitary forces are focused 100 percent of their time on counterterrorism. On the other hand, the regular military forces and local police departments do not focus on one task but, instead, cover a myriad of defense and public safety tasks.

Distract the In-country Isfast Terrorists. We have seen that Mohamed Atta (who helped bring down the WTC) could down heavy liquor. Indeed, he prided himself in being able to out-drink all others. We should take advantage of this type of Achilles heel. We should provide these terrorists with ample wine and later, women. We saw that the terrorists would stare at the scantily dressed women around the swimming pool. Thus, even though they have their strict religious codes, they are still tempted to drink and look at women. Attempt to sidetrack them with female Arabic espionage agents to break down their morals and use illicit sex as a weapon. *Distract Isfasts from their focus on destruction by causing them to "take their eyes off the ball."*

> *Distract Isfasts from their focus on destruction by causing them to "take their eyes of the ball."*

Identification Tags. Register and have all AMI foreigners in the United States carry an identification tag. Fingerprint, photograph, and keep a database on all of them.

Informants. Develop AMI informants to provide police with knowledge of suspected terrorists in our midst. Pay informants whatever it takes to acquire good information from them.

Urban Warfare. Conduct urban warfare. Urban warfare is warfare in the city. Isfast terror cells exist in many of the major cities throughout the United States and the world. Charge our paramilitary force to take them out one at a time … quietly and without any fanfare. *Get the Isfasts to shoot first. Then terminate their lives with silencers. That would be the easiest way to be-rid of them. We should eliminate the step that stalls their disposal through our currently screwed-up US justice system.*

> *Get the Isfasts to shoot first. Then terminate their lives with silencers. That would be the easiest way to be-rid of them. We should eliminate the step that stalls their disposal through our currently screwed-up US justice system.*

Doomsday/Armageddon Strategy

Massive Retaliation or MAD. Should Doomsday ever come upon us, massive retaliation, or Mutually Assured Destruction (MAD), is the best and only way to go.

Anything and Everything Goes. Should we ever get to the point of our annihilation and/or being conquered, we then shall employ every strategy and tactic available in our repertoire. These "free-for-all" strategies/tactics include the following:

- First strike
- Massive retaliation, MAD
- Scorched earth (carpet bombing)
- Level all major enemy cities with tactical nuclear weapons (blow them back to the Stone Ages)
- Assassinations of enemy political and military leaders
- Beheadings
- Torture (Far Eastern, Oriental style)
- Collateral damage
- Fratricide if required to get top enemy leaders
- Human suicide bombers
- Kamikaze bombers
- WMDs (chemical warfare, germ warfare, and nuclear/radiological warfare)
- Nuclear holocaust
- Genocide (mass murder)
- Totally destroy all enemy infrastructure
- Crops eradication
- Kill all livestock and other animals

- Poison all water supplies
- Leave no person standing (kill all enemy military and civilian personnel), i.e., *apply the "take absolutely no prisoners" policy*
- Use whatever new strategies and tactics that come to mind

> *Apply the "take absolutely no prisoners" policy.*

Chapter 6

Military Tactics to Counter Isfasts

The *American Heritage® Dictionary* defines *tactics* as the military science that deals with securing objectives set by strategy, especially the technique of deploying and directing troops, ships, and aircraft in effective maneuvers against an enemy; a procedure or set of maneuvers engaged in to achieve an end, an aim, or a goal.

Tactics are subsets of strategy. Accomplishing a number of relevant tactics achieves a related strategy. Objectives are subsets of a goal. Accomplishing a number of relevant objectives achieves a related goal. Hence, tactics are to objectives as strategies are to goals. They are all interrelated.

Regarding tactics, General George S. Patton said, "*Good tactics can save even the worst strategy. Bad tactics will destroy even the best strategy.*" How true ring his words! There is absolutely no doubt in my mind that General Patton was the greatest military general, strategist, and warrior America has ever produced. All of the following military tactics are available for employment in our asymmetrical wars.

> *Good tactics can save even the worst strategy. Bad tactics will destroy even the best strategy.*
>
> **General George S. Patton, Jr.**

Lightning Warfare Tactic

Blitzkrieg (lightning war), or surprise, works well in battle. The Germans used this tactic effectively in World War II. Sun Tzu said, "*Let your plans be dark and impenetrable as night, and when you move, fall like a thunderbolt.*"[44] He was talk-

---

44.   Sun Tzu, *The Art of War*. Extracted on 10/15/06 from The Internet Classics Archive of the Massachusetts Institute of Technology at the following URL: http://classics.mit.edu/Tzu/artwar.html.

ing about lightning warfare or *blitzkrieg*. The Germans learned well from Sun Tzu.

Ambush Tactic

Ambush the enemy is a good tactic to employ along with "shock and awe." The element of surprise is always effective in putting the enemy on the defensive. Ambushing an enemy is always better than confronting him head-on. Always choose ambush over a frontal attack.

Deception Tactic

Use deception in dealing with the Isfast enemy. Make extensive use of feigned weaknesses, camouflage, stealth technology, disinformation, and decoys. Sun Tzu said, "*All warfare is based on deception. Hence, when able to attack, we must seem unable. When using our forces, we must seem inactive. When we are near, we must make the enemy believe we are far away. When far away, we must make him believe we are near. Hold out baits to entice the enemy. Feign disorder and [then] crush him.*"[45] We must listen to Sun Tzu!

Dress as the Enemy Tactic

Dress our troops in the same uniforms as that of the enemy, i.e., street clothes, *burkas*, head wraps, robes, long beards, and dirty/scruffy appearance. This provides good personal camouflage and is effective in clandestine operations within enemy territory. Remember, *in asymmetrical warfare, the side with the simplest uniforms wins*. The simplest uniforms are dirty street clothes.

> *In asymmetrical warfare, the side with the simplest uniforms wins.*

Infiltration Tactic

Infiltrate terrorist cells and enemy forces. Establish moles in their cells and forces. If John Walker can become a Taliban, why cannot anyone else fake their conversion to Islam and join the various Isfast organizations (al-Qaida, Taliban,

---

45.   Ibid.

Hamas, and Hezbolla)? We should recruit good, loyal American-AMIs to become infiltrating CIA or other agents as moles. We need to apply the same tactics on them as they apply on us.

Military Tribunal Tactic

Give the captured Isfast terrorists the same quality of trial that our captive soldiers receive from them. Fair is fair. Hold secret military tribunals to try accused Isfast terrorists. After found guilty, they should be quietly hanged, executed before a firing squad, injected with a poison serum, electrocuted on the electric chair, or cut off their heads with the same kind of weapon they use to cut

> *All is fair in love and war.*

off our soldiers' heads. Isfast terrorists are *de facto* (not officially recognized) military combatants who do not deserve the full run of constitutional rights. *All is fair in love and war.*

Improvised Explosive Devices Tactic

Use improvised explosive devices (IEDs) of our own against al-Qaida, Taliban, Hezbollah, Hamas, Iran, Syria, and North Korea. If they can effectively use IEDs against us, we can effectively use IEDs against them … except we can provide a whole lot more firepower … 10 times more.

Suicide Bombers Tactic

Use suicide bombers against all of our enemies that use them against us. In our country, we have whackos also that would do anything for money even if it went to their next of kin. Should we get to a point of being conquered, pull all stops; use suicide bombers just as they do. What is there to lose at this point? Fight fire with fire.

Decapitation Tactic

Use decapitation techniques as used by the enemy. Perhaps chain saws would work more effectively than dull knife blades. Film the decapitation and send the

CD to al-Jazeera and the Communist News Network (CNN). Fight fire with fire.

Revenge Tactic

Should we seek revenge for the dastardly deed the Osama bin Laden's terrorists did to the World Trade Center Twin Towers and the nearly 3,000 innocent civilians that he had slaughtered? What should we do? General Patton said, "*When you put your hand into a bunch of goo, that a moment before was your best friend's face, you'll know what to do.*" When this happens to you, revenge comes readily to mind.

Booby Traps Tactic

Use booby traps to get the Isfast terrorists. The Vietcong used it well in the war in Southeast Asia. We should do likewise to the Isfast terrorists.

Get Osama bin Laden Tactic

Establish, dedicate, and assign two specially trained military divisions to find, capture, and/or kill Osama bin Laden as their sole mission in life. They must accomplish that mission within 12 months from the go-ahead. If we decapitate the head, we slow down the movement. When strongman totalitarian leaders die, what happens to their political/ideological movements? Their movements usually slow down for a while until and if another strong, fanatical leader surfaces. Examples of these killer leaders include Adolph Hitler, Joseph Stalin, Mao Tse-tung, Ho Chi Minh, Ayatollah Ruhollah Khomeini, and recently demised Saddam Hussein and terminally ill Fidel Castro. Better days are ahead of us.

> **Establish, dedicate, and assign two specially trained military divisions to find, capture, and/or kill Osama bin Laden as their sole mission in life.**

Target and Kill Five Evil Hitlers Tactic

Better That a Few Evil Men Perish. Target and kill Hitler of the world Osama bin Laden, Hitler of Iraq Saddam Hussein (done deal), Hitler of Iran Mahmoud Ahmadinejad, Hitler of Venezuela Hugo Chavez, and Hitler of North Korea Kim Jong Il. *It is better that a few evil men perish than entire nations dwindle and perish because of these evil men's dastardly ideologies, philosophies, and deeds.*

Never Capture an Evil Leader Alive. We should have never captured Hitler Saddam Hussein. His captors should have shot him dead when he exited his spider hole. Look at the silly kangaroo court that went on with him. It was such a farce! We should have quickly tried, convicted, and hanged him from the nearest tree.

> *It is better that a few evil men perish than entire nations dwindle and perish because of these evil men's dastardly ideologies, philosophies, and deeds.*

Death of Slobodan Milosevic. Even though the Iraq court has sentenced him to death, maybe he could have received the same fate as former Yugoslav leader Slobodan Milosevic, the first head of state indicted for war crimes. He mysteriously died in his cell at The Hague. A report from his lawyer said that someone might have poisoned Milosevic. However, the public prosecutor concluded that Hitler Milosevic died of natural causes, and that there were no indications that his death had resulted from crime. Yeah, right! That should have been the same fate of Hitler Saddam Hussein. However, the Iraqis hanged him instead. Good!

Kidnap and Destroy Tactic

Kidnap and eradicate their leaders. Assassinate Isfast terrorist leaders and leaders of countries that support terrorism. Use the "cloak and dagger" approach. Poison their food. That is what the alleged Russians did to Alexander Litvinenko, a former KGB agent. Polonium-210 worked just fine in snuffing out this man. Litvinenko, 43, told police he was poisoned on November 1 while investigating the October gun slaying of Russian journalist Anna Politkovskaya, another critic of Putin's government.[46]

Create Uprisings Tactics

Generate uprisings in countries that support Isfast terrorists. Get the masses to overturn the leadership of those countries and initiate regime change.

Propaganda Tactic

Spread propaganda to win the hearts and minds of the people of these rogue nations and to combat Isfast terrorists. "Propaganda" is the systematic propagation of a doctrine or cause or of information reflecting the views and interests of its propagators (United States).

Groundhog Tactic

After the Isfast terrorists seek refuge in their mountain caves and tunnels, smoke them out as you would a groundhog. Find out where the entrances, exits, and air holes are located. Then, use poison gas, tear gas, and regular smoke to smoke them out or fill the tunnels with water or some other solvent to drown them. Fill the entrances with large boulders and concrete them in. An alternative could be to dynamite the entrances and exits. The cave-ins would seal the enemy inside their caves and tunnels.

Front Organizations Tactic

Set up front organizations such as gun and ammunition stores, military weapons stores, and explosives stores to lure Isfast terrorists in to purchase these goods. Take photos of them using hidden cameras and record their voices using hidden microphones or bugs (clandestine electronic devices). Use the information they provide and set up a dossier on them. Monitor them to gather hard evidence of their terror-related activities.

---

46.   David Stringer, Associated Press Writer, "Dying Spy Said to Accuse Russian Agent." Extracted on 11/25/06 from *Yahoo! News* at URL: http://news.yahoo.com/s/ap/20061126/ap_on_re_eu/britain_poisoned_spy.

Hostages Tactic

Take hostages just like the terrorists do. Capture Osama bin Laden's wife, children, and other relatives and use them as bargaining chips to get at Osama. However, do not be surprised if he sacrifices them for his own cause. Sun Tzu said, "*If asked how to cope with a great host of the enemy in orderly array and on the point of marching to the attack, I should say: 'Begin by seizing something which your opponent holds dear; then he will be amenable to your will.'*"[47] That means using hostages.

Nullify al-Jazeera Tactic

Bomb all al-Jazeera facilities and level them to the ground. Al-Jazeera currently serves as a propaganda tool of the Islamo-fascist terrorists. They are part of the enemy infrastructure. Hence, we should destroy al-Jazeera NOW! Next, we should dismantle the Communist News Network (CNN). CNN is a sister station of al-Jazeera.

> *Bomb all al-Jazeera facilities and level them to the ground.*

No Negotiating with Tribal Cleric Leaders Tactic

I have heard repeated stories about tribal opposition leaders negotiating the surrender of Taliban and al-Qaida leaders such as Mullah Omar and others (for three times now), which only resulted in the rascals getting away. The first time we made that mistake, shame on you. The second time we made that mistake, shame on us. However, the third time we made that mistake … ! When are we ever going to learn that we cannot trust those Pashtun tribal cleric leaders? They were not negotiating; they were stalling for time for those al-Qaida and Taliban rascals to escape!

Our military leaders must take over all negotiations and get those untrustworthy Afghan leaders out of the negotiating business. If we do not do that, we will not find Mullah Omar and Osama bin Laden for a very long time.

---

47. Sun Tzu, *The Art of War*. Extracted on 10/15/06 from The Internet Classics Archive of the Massachusetts Institute of Technology at URL: http://classics.mit.edu/Tzu/artwar.html.

Mosque Tactic

Whenever we identify an Islamic mosque that serves as a sanctuary and harbors Isfast terrorists or stores military weaponry, we bomb and level it to the ground. Right now, all the Catholic Pope has to do is to make the mild statement he did in a classroom environment, and the offended Isfasts have burned down hundreds of Christian churches. What's wrong with that picture? By their actions, we do not need to be careful about avoiding mosques any longer. If it is suspected to house terrorists, we level it to the ground. Fair is fair.

> *Whenever we identify an Islamic mosque that serves as a sanctuary and harbors Isfast terrorists or stores military weaponry, we bomb and level it to the ground.*

Sniper Tactic

Use sharp-shooting snipers with 50-caliber rifles to kill Isfast terrorists and suspected terrorist and those who support terrorism. We should have detained the Iranian Hitler when he dared to put his foot on our New York soil to give his vitriolic speech against the US at the United Nations.

Do you think our president would have survived making a visit to Tehran, Iran, to give such a vitriolic speech to the Iranians? Fat chance! We would have had a dead president on our hands.

Confrontation with Iran will occur sooner or later. It is better to do it sooner rather than later. Hence, we should do it soon or it is going to be too late.

> *Confrontation with Iran will occur sooner or later. It is better to do it sooner rather than later.*

Bounty Hunters Tactic

Hire bounty hunters, offering them very lucrative bounties (in the hundreds of millions of dollars), to go after Osama bin Laden, his lieutenants, and other Isfast terrorists.

Mafia Tactic

Hire the Mafia to kill terrorists in the United States. Use silencers to shoot terrorists in our cities.

Mercenaries and Militiamen Tactic

Hire mercenaries and militiamen to go after Osama bin Laden. Hire "hit men" or use "hit squads" to pursue the Isfast terrorists. Hire the Rambo bounty hunters out there. There are many of them around just looking for a fight and money. Money motivates, particularly when there are lots of it. Use proxy Afghan forces to go after the Isfast terrorists. In other words, *use their own kind to get their kind.*

> *Use their own kind to get their kind.*

Reward Tactic

Instead of $25 million, *offer a reward of $100 million to any individual or group who kills Osama bin Laden and brings in his corpse and/or head.* Distribute "Wanted Dead-or-Alive" posters, fliers, and signs. Airdrop leaflets over countries where he is suspected to be hiding. Additionally, offer and pay anyone $1 million for every proven terrorist that they can kill or get arrested, tried, convicted, and executed. They must deliver the corpse and/or head to a designated location to claim their reward.

Sabotage Tactic

Get our crack, elite units to commit sabotage on all of the assets of value in Afghanistan, Iraq, Lebanon, Iran, North Korea, and Syria. Hire mercenary saboteurs to knock off Isfast terrorists, their assets, and other targets of opportunity.

> *Offer a reward of $100 million to any individual or group who kills Osama bin Laden and brings in his corpse and/or head.*

Torture Tactic

Always Keep Torture as an Available Weapon of War. If the enemy uses torture, we should not discard it just because we are a civilized society. If we took it to the limit, we may become an extinct, civilized society. That may be our ultimate destiny if we do not take the necessary and sufficient actions when we come to a do-or-die moment. So, do not ever discount it

> *Water boarding should be the most desirable of these motivation tactics.*

as a potential tool of warfare. Should we approach our country's demise, we must fight fire with fire, or we lose.

Water Boarding. Apply the severest means possible to squeeze out confidential information from captured/arrested Isfast terrorists including the use of Far Eastern torture techniques and injected truth serum. *Water boarding should be the most desirable of these motivation tactics.*

The Debate Goes on Forever. During 2006, a big debate continued among political and intelligence communities about: What constitutes torture? If there could be a dichotomy, what constitutes bad torture and what constitutes acceptable torture? The debate will continue to go on long after someone publishes and distributes a document showing the definition of "torture." I like the approach that President Teddy Roosevelt took as illustrated in his following quote: *"I took the Canal Zone and let Congress debate; and while the debate goes on, the canal does too."*[48]

Do Not Exclude Torture from the Survival Equation. Let the politicians and talking heads debate about "torture." In the meantime, the President of the United States has a job to do, which is to protect the lives and safety of the American people. *To annihilate the Isfasts before they annihilate us, we must do whatever is required to main-*

> *To annihilate the Isfasts before they annihilate us, we must do whatever is required to maintain our continued survival, or we will be conquered and placed in bondage.*

48.   Theodore Roosevelt, "Teddy Roosevelt Quotes," as extracted on 9/13/06 from URL http://www.teddyroosevelt.com/deddy_roosevelt_quotes.htm.

tain our continued survival, or we will be conquered and placed in bondage. Yes, we must not exclude even torture from the survival equation. Hence, torture must go on by the "doers" even while the "talkers" debate the "torture" word to death *ad infinitum.*

Prepare for the Coming Isfast Terrorist Attacks

Personal and Family Preparation. Personally, we must be alert, vigilant, and prepared for Isfast terrorist attacks, which are sure to come. Everyone can take care of self and family by doing the following:

- Keep in good health (proper exercise, rest, diet, and physical exams).
- Be current in your family shots and immunizations.
- Prepare a 72-hour emergency kit for your home and/or car.
- Establish a food storage program (year's supply) in your home.
- Keep the cars sufficiently gassed; never go below 1/4 tank of gas.
- Purchase and use cell/digital/wireless/satellite phones, BlackBerries, and/or CB radio.
- Raise, train, and use pigeons for communications (for those living in rural areas).
- Purchase and store in your homes sufficient flashlights, dry cell batteries, candles, waterproof matches, bottled water, duct tape, and plastic wrap.
- Prepare a plan to evacuate your home and conduct drills/exercises.
- Prepare a plan to communicate with all members of your family (particularly if you are a family with members spread across the country).
- Read scriptures and stay close to your God (no matter what faith you claim).
- Purchase and have available in your home a transistor radio.
- Purchase and have available in your home a good first-aid kit.

- *Be vigilant and aware of what goes on around you.*

- Report to the police anybody acting strangely or suspiciously.

- Keep emergency services (police, fire, ambulance, paramedics, and doctor) phone numbers handy for ready reference.

> *Be vigilant and aware of what goes on around you.*

- Keep aware of the news regarding the War on Terrorism and other major events occurring in the world and country.

- Own a dog or two for protecting your yard and home. Even little dogs will provide sufficient warning by barking loudly.

- Keep a fire extinguisher in your home and know how to use it.

- Keep a good set of tools handy in your home.

- Keep a sufficient amount of cash handy.

- Put dead bolts on the exit doors of your home.

- Create a safe room in the home where all members of the family can find the most safety and security.

- Purchase and have available rope, cable, and/or chains (with strength to handle 100 lb more than planned and length more than 100 ft longer than required) for emergency use.

- Keep a para-glider handy (if you are a para-glider enthusiast and work in a very tall skyscraper).

Be Prepared. These are just a few of the things that every citizen of this country can do to be prepared for any emergency whether it be a natural disaster (earthquake, tidal wave, tornado, storm, hurricane, wildfire, or volcano eruption), riots, arson, burglary, vandalism, shootout, war, terrorist attack, or whatever. Most people do not even have half of these things accomplished or available in their homes for their families.

Understand WMDs. As citizens, we need to know about CBR (chemical, biological, and radiological) and NBC (nuclear, biological, and chemical) weapons, whichever the terminology people use. We also need to think about dealing with weapons of mass destruction (WMD) such as chemical or gas warfare (poisonous gas), biological or germ warfare (deadly germs, diseases, and plagues), nuclear warfare (flash and heat from the blast, flying debris, and residual radioactivity), and radiological warfare (dirty bombs; radioactive waste).

Don't Stick Your Head in the Sand. We need to think about gas masks. We need to think about immunizations and antidotes to combat diseases, illnesses, and radioactive poisoning. We need to think about bomb shelters and body protective gear (e.g., helmets and bulletproof vests). We need to think about defensive personal weaponry (guns and ammunition). *We must not "stick our heads in the sand" as do the ostriches.*

> *We must not "stick our heads in the sand" as do the ostriches.*

Our Infrastructure Needs Better Protection. Our schools, hospitals, and strategic resources are insufficiently prepared for such a major event as an Isfast terrorist attack using WMD. Our nuclear power plants need better protection. Our water supplies, livestock, and farmlands need better protection. Our electrical power generating stations and national power grid need better protection. Our bridges, tunnels, dams, petroleum storage tanks, cross-country gas lines, and radio/TV stations need better protection. Our communications and Internet infrastructure need better protection. Our ships and seaports need better protection. *Currently, we sufficiently protect only our airports and aircraft.*

> *Currently, we sufficiently protect only our airports and aircraft.*

Be Prepared for the Isfast Attacks. Hence, the people must actively work to protect themselves. When the terrorists hit a dozen or more of our major cities simultaneously this year or next, panic will break out. This panic condition will prevail until some sort or order is restored. Restoring order is the responsibility of the Department of Defense (DoD), National Guard, Department of Homeland Security, Coast Guard, Federal Emergency Management Agency (FEMA), civilian law enforcement (police), fire department, and anyone else involved in antiterrorism and counterterrorism. I hope everyone will

> *The only thing to fear is fear itself.*
>
> **President Franklin D. Roosevelt**

prepare themselves for these pending attacks. Remember this: when you are prepared, you need not fear.

If Prepared, No Need to Fear. My recommendation to you and all of your friends is not to delay any longer if they have not prepared any for this War on Terrorism. Do not get caught by surprise. Know exactly what can happen and what you can do about it. The Boy Scout motto is "Be prepared." So, remember this: When you are prepared, you don't need to fear anything. President Franklin D. Roosevelt said, "*The only thing to fear is fear itself.*"

Chapter 7

High-Tech Concepts to Counter Isfasts

High-tech equipment and weaponry have its place in the fight against terrorism. It is not the panacea to the problem. However, used properly and effectively, it serves a purpose in the War on Terror. We should use 7th Century strategies and tactics against the Isfasts. However, we should not revert back to 7th Century weapons and equipment. Our high-tech equipment and weaponry can and will outperform the state of technology currently being used by the Isfasts. We must continually stay ahead of the technology they employ.

Aircraft Security

Black Box. Because a plane crash can destroy or lose the "black box," it is now obsolete. *We must upgrade the black box to transmit automatically in real time the conversations that occur during crises, accidents, or incidents.* The signals should be transmitted to both satellite and ground station transceivers and have the conversations recorded and relayed to the FBI, police, air traffic control (ATC), and Federal Aviation Administration (FAA) as incidents/accidents occur.

> *We must upgrade the black box to transmit automatically in real time the conversations that occur during crisis, accidents, or incidents.*

Doors to Pilot's Cabin. Develop high-security doors for aircraft. Explosion proof these doors to the pilot's cabin. Make those doors lock from the inside with a deadbolt and door bar.

De-arming System. When the warning system warns the pilot that terrorists are on board in the passenger cabin, the pilot presses a button that quickly sprays sleeping gas throughout the entire passenger cabin. This system must be a secretly installed so that nobody knows about it … particularly the Isfast terrorists. All passengers (including terrorists) will quickly fall asleep (become unconscious). The wall/door to the cockpit must be gas proof sealed. The pilot lands the plane, and police arrest the terrorists. This must be a clandestine system. Carry-on bags shall not include gas masks. The passenger cabin includes installed, hidden closed-circuit television (CCTV) cameras so that the pilot could see on an instrument panel screen what is occurring back in the passenger cabin.

Cockpit System. Install in the cockpit a system that gives out very high-pitch, eardrum-piercing sound waves (high decibels) both in the cabin and through the earphones that would destroy the terrorists' hearing and cause unbearable pain once they kill the pilots and close the cabin door. The system, which uses a two-minute delay, could be activated by the ground controller (air traffic controller), by the chief stewardess, or by the plane's captain just prior to his being disabled by the terrorist.

If the terrorist hold their hands to their ears, they will be unable to use their hands to steer the plane or manipulate any of the knobs and switches on the instrument panel. The plane will eventually crash. In the event the terrorists were prepared with earplugs, a backup system would release tear gas, sleeping (anesthesia) gas, and/or poisonous gas to disable the terrorists operating in the cockpit. The plane will eventually crash.

Warning System. Develop a warning system in aircraft for passengers to be able to press a button to warn the pilot of an on-board terrorist.

Voice Activation to Incapacitate Hijacking Terrorists. Install in the aircraft cockpit an Arabic voice-activated system. This system consists of one or a combination of any of the following six approaches:

- Releases poisonous gas,
- Shoots bullets from a hidden gun in the instrument panel to the pilot's position in the seat,
- Releases a bright flash of light that temporarily blinds the terrorist for at least five minutes,
- Decompresses the cockpit,
- Releases an eardrum piercing sound, or
- Explodes a hand grenade-type bomb that releases an excessive amount of shrapnel.

Building Protection

Skyscrapers. Strengthen the building of skyscrapers so that they will not implode, buckle, or progressively collapse from a fire within the building.

Cyber Security

Internet. Use the Internet to track down and monitor all computers and laptops used by Isfast terrorists.

Hackers. Use hackers to garble the Isfast terrorist messages transmitted through communications systems and computers.

Detection Devices

CB Warfare Agent Detectors. Develop high-technology sniffers that will be able to detect and identify deadly chemical and biological agents used by Isfast terrorists for mass murder/destruction.

Electronic Scanning Devices. Use electronic scanners to detect nonmetal weapons and explosives.

Face Scanning Devices. Use face-scanning devices to match faces in crowds to Isfast terrorist databases.

Hand and/or Finger Scanning Devices. Use hand and/or finger scanning devices to match persons in crowds to Isfast terrorist databases.

Lie Detectors. Put arrested or captured suspected Isfast terrorists through a battery of lie detector tests. If they fail the tests, bingo! We may have a hot prospect to interrogate even further.

Metal Detection. Develop better metal detectors.

MRI. Use magnetic resonance imaging (MRI) technology for weapons detection.

Night Vision. Use night vision equipment to search out and identify Isfast terrorists at night.

Non-Metallic Weapons Detection. Develop detectors that can identify non-metallic (e.g., plastic, liquid, and gel) weapons on the body, in carry-on bags, and in suitcases.

Retina Scanner. Use retina scanners to identify people that enter high-security, high-value facilities that may be Isfast terrorist targets.

Smart Cards. Replace paper passports with plastic smart cards that encode personal information and hand, finger, face, or retina scans. Match Isfast terrorists with data in an Isfast terrorist database.

Voice Recognition. Use voice recognition devices to identify people that enter high-security, high-value facilities that may be Isfast terrorist targets.

X-Ray. Improve the X-ray machines to identify weapons (box cutters, knives, and guns).

Listening Devices

Bugs. Use bugs and other listening devices (electronic surveillance) to intercept conversations and wireless phone calls.

Eavesdropping Devices. Develop better and more effective eavesdropping devices that evade being seen, detected, and/or countered. Embed microminiaturized eavesdropping devices on humans, animals, and equipment so that we can hear sensitive conversations and accumulate data for conducting military actions on the enemy.

Sensors

Motion Sensing. Use motion sensors for detecting intruding Isfast terrorists.

Vibration Sensing. Use vibration sensor technology for identifying intruding Isfast terrorists.

Surveillance Systems

Spy Satellites. Use our spy satellites to track individual Isfast terrorists.

Surveillance. Use space surveillance to identify, track, and pinpoint Isfast terrorists, cells, and terrorist camps.

Spy Planes. Conduct spy plane flights over Afghanistan, Iraq, and other Isfast terrorist supporting countries to gather needed information to conduct successful military operations.

Unmanned Aerial Vehicles (UAVs). Use UAVs on reconnaissance flights to photograph Isfast terrorist camps. Use UAVs as *kamikaze* vehicles/bombs on

Isfast terrorist camps and cells. Position UAVs 90,000 feet above coastlines to sense Isfast terrorist and their missiles.

Translation Devices

Scanner-Translator. Develop a scanner-translator to translate hard copies of documents written in Arabic languages into English.

Translating. Develop software systems for real-time, accurate translating of Arabic languages into English when wiretapping, listening to wireless phone calls, and intercepting e-mail and faxes.

Weapons

Miyamoto Musashi said, "*There is a time and place for use of weapons.*"[49] We should use all available weapons for appropriate targets of opportunity. Furthermore, Musashi said, "*You should not have a favorite weapon. To become over-familiar with one weapon is as much a fault as not knowing it sufficiently well. You should not copy others, but use weapons that you can handle properly. It is bad for commanders and troopers to have likes and dislikes. These are things you must learn thoroughly.*"[50]

Cruise Missiles. Use cruise missiles to bomb Isfast terrorist camps.

Laser Weapons. Develop laser guns to zap Isfast terrorists from space satellites and space stations.

Paraphernalia. Develop cutting-edge, high technology paraphernalia (i.e., equipment, devices, documents, gadgets, tools, and weapons) used in clandestine missions to trick, attack, or demoralize Isfast terrorists. These paraphernalia may include such things as:

- Grenades that explode on impact instead of being on a timer,
- Compass in a clothes button,
- Miniature pistol that can be concealed easily,
- Caltrops for puncturing tires,

---

49.   Miyamoto Musashi, *A Book of Five Rings*, "*Go Rin No Sho.*" Extracted on 10/13/06 from http://www.miyamotomusashi.com/gorin.htm.

50.   Ibid.

- Maps concealed in decks of cards,
- Silent pistols,
- Limpet (clings to the hull) mines with acetone time-delay fuses to use against ships,
- Miniature cameras that could fit into a matchbox,
- Two-man kayaks,
- "Aunt Jemima" explosive powder packages in Chinese flour bags, and
- Inconspicuous letter-drops.

Other paraphernalia may include:
- Wiretap devices,
- Electronic beacons for field agents,
- Portable radios to allow agents to communicate securely with an aircraft circling high overhead,
- Fabricated documents (e.g., passports, ration cards, work passes, ID cards, and occupation currency),
- Specialized boats, equipment, and explosives,
- Underwater breathing gear,
- Waterproof watches and compasses,
- Inflatable motorized surfboard, and
- Remote-controlled speedboat guided by aircraft.

No idea should be overlooked however unorthodox, ridiculous, or untried.

Stealth. Use the stealth bombers and stealth fighters to attack at night and bomb Isfast terrorist camps.

Guided Bombs. Use satellite-guided bombs launched from warplanes for getting at the Isfast terrorist camps and other targets of value.

> *No idea should be overlooked however unorthodox, ridiculous, or untried.*

CBR Warfare. Use chemical/gas (poison gas), biological/germ, and radiological/nuclear warfare on the Isfast terrorists after they use these weapons first.

Natural and Synthetic Agents. Use natural and synthetic agents such as diseases and cultures ranging from exotic anthrax to commonplace, but just as deadly, scourges like the foot-and-mouth epidemic that recently swept Europe. Other agents that we can use include smallpox, pneumonic plague, ebola, and other viral hemorrhagic fevers. If the Isfast terrorists use these agents, use it back on them.

Deadly Gas. Use sarin gas, botulin toxin, and nerve gas to fight Isfast terrorists.

Defoliants. Use defoliating agents on their crops to starve the Isfast terrorist population.

Cluster Bombs. Use the BL 755 cluster bomb, an area-impact weapon employed by the Royal Air Force's (RAF's) Harriers. Each bomb contains 147 grenade-sized "bomblets" that disperse over an area the size of half a football field. Each bomblet detonates producing up to 2,000 high-velocity shrapnel fragments. The effect is similar to a large number of miniature nail bombs exploding simultaneously. The USAF has a similar weapon, the BCU87B, that contains 202 bomblets. We dropped more than 10,000 of these bombs during the 1991 Gulf War.

Crossbows. Use Rambo-style crossbows for hunting and killing Isfast terrorists in the mountains of Afghanistan.

Fuel-Air Bombs. Use fuel-air explosive bombs, which are more devastating than conventional bombs. These bombs succeed the napalm, though typically, they cover a wider area and disperse more evenly. Sun Tzu said, "*There are five ways of attacking with fire:*

- *The first is to burn soldiers in their camp.*
- *The second is to burn stores.*
- *The third is to burn baggage trains.*
- *The fourth is to burn arsenals and magazines.*
- *And the fifth is to hurl dropping fire amongst the enemy.*"

This last bullet is analogous to dropping fuel-air bombs today.

Slurry Bombs. Use this very powerful bomb weighing nearly seven tons and capable of producing blast-effects of up to 1,000 psi, not much less than a small tactical nuclear weapon.

Napalm Surpluses. Use up the old, surplus napalm on Isfast terrorist camps.

Land Mines. Use more land mines to get the Isfast terrorists. Mine door-knobs, TV sets, and cigarette packages that lay on the ground. Blow off a hand or two.

Missiles. Use surface-to-air missiles (SAMs) and shoulder-fired Stinger missiles to get the Isfast terrorists.

Silencers. Use silencers to shoot Isfast terrorists in terror cells throughout the world.

Tactical Nuclear Weapons. Use tactical nuclear weapons on the Isfast terrorist training camps.

Surplus Nuclear Weapons. Use up our old nuclear bombs on Isfast terrorist camps.

Chapter 8

Good Intelligence—Key to Victory

Intelligence is Key

Good military and civilian intelligence is the key to winning 21st Century wars. The most important kind of intelligence is human intelligence (HUMINT). We need to pay good money for valuable information provided to us by the AMI people willing to sell us the gathered G-2. Money talks. *Follow the money trail.* There will always be someone ready to take a fist full of money for good information. *Feed greed.*

> **Feed greed.**
> **Follow the**
> **money trail.**

Sun Tzu said, *"Thus, what enables the wise sovereign and the good general to strike and conquer and achieve things beyond the reach of ordinary men is foreknowledge. Now, spirits cannot elicit this foreknowledge. We cannot obtain it inductively from experience or by any deductive calculation. We can obtain knowledge of the enemy's dispositions only from other men."*[51]

Intelligence Sources & Methods

Conduct full-scale intelligence on Islamo-fascists (Isfasts) using all available sources, forms, and methods. Do not let anything pass by without analysis. Do not allow anything to hamper the operations. As Admiral David Glasgow Farragut (1801-1870) said, *"Damn the torpedoes; full speed ahead!"*

> **Damn the torpedoes;**
> **full speed ahead!**
> **Adm. David Farragut**

---

51. Sun Tzu, *The Art of War*. Extracted on 10/15/06 from The Internet Classics Archive of the Massachusetts Institute of Technology at URL: http://classics.mit.edu/Tzu/artwar.html.

Human Intelligence (HUMINT)

Human Intelligence (HUMINT) is the most important sources and methods we can use to acquire high-value intelligence on the Islamo-fascists (Isfasts). Develop our HUMINT capability to gather current, important data on Isfasts. Assign intelligence analysts and operators to gather, organize, analyze, use, and store Isfast intelligence data and information. *Leverage Pakistani Intelligence to kill Isfasts and, in particular, Osama bin Laden.*

> *Leverage Pakistani Intelligence to kill Isfasts and, in particular, Osama bin Laden.*

Sun Tzu said, "*Spies include the following five classes:*

- *Local spies—employing the services of the inhabitants of a district*

- *Inward spies—making use of officials of the enemy*

- *Converted spies—getting hold of the enemy's spies and using them for our own purposes*

- *Doomed spies—doing certain things openly for purposes of deception and allowing our spies to know of them and report them to the enemy*

- *Surviving spies—those who bring back news from the enemy's camp*"[52]

Hence, maintain more intimate relations with spies than with anyone else in the whole army. Liberally reward spies but not others. In no other business should we preserve greater secrecy.[53]

Recruit American Arabs/Muslims/Islamites

The FBI and CIA should recruit American Arabs/Muslims/Islamites (AMIs) (those who prove to be true, loyal Americans) to become translators, intelligence/counterintelligence agents (or espionage agents) to infiltrate and spy on the enemy as Isfast terrorist cell moles. They will dress, look, speak, and act like the enemy ... except they will be on our side to bring back valuable G-2 for us to use to exterminate the enemy.

---

52.   Ibid.
53.   Ibid.

Recruit Trustworthy, Indigenous AMIs to Acquire Isfast Terrorists G-2

Hire trustworthy, indigenous AMIs from various countries in the Middle East and pay them well for good HUMINT, which is very important to win the war. They must have absolutely no allegiance to the Isfast terrorists. Give them bonuses for especially good information that helps the US to capture or destroy the key Isfast leaders.

Racial Profiling

Apply racial profiling to ferret out the thousands of enemy Isfast sleepers already residing within the US. Look at the following:

Year	Event
1968	Bobby Kennedy shot and killed
1972	Jewish athletes kidnapped and massacred at the Munich Olympics
1979	US embassy in Iran taken over
1980s	A number of Americans kidnapped in Lebanon
1983	US Marine barracks in Beirut, Lebanon, blown up killing over 200 US marines
1985	Cruise ship Achilles Lauro hijacked and a 70-year-old American passenger in a wheelchair murdered and thrown overboard
1985	TWA flight 847 hijacked at Athens, Greece, and a US Navy diver murdered while attempting to rescue the passengers
1988	Pan Am Flight 103 bombed
1993	World Trade Center bombed the first time
1998	US embassies in Kenya and Tanzania bombed
2001	Four airliners hijacked; two used as missiles to take out the World Trade Center; and of the remaining two, one crashed into the US Pentagon and the other diverted and crashed by the passengers in a Pennsylvania field
2002	The US fought a war in Afghanistan

2002	Reporter Daniel Pearl kidnapped and beheaded
2004	Spain railway bombings occurred
2005	London subway bombings occurred
2006	Plot to blow up airliners leaving London for the US

Profiling is Justified. This chronological list of facts indicates a pattern. The underlying, common thread that weaves through all of these events is that all of these events involved extremist Muslim males or Isfasts mostly between the ages of 17 and 40. The pattern you see here justifies profiling. However, look at what Secretary of Transportation did.

> *The pattern you see here justifies profiling.*

Secretary Norm Mineta Refused to Allow Profiling. Dr. Vernon Chong, Major General, USAF, Retired, said, "*Let me give you a few examples of how we simply do not comprehend the life and death seriousness of this situation. President Bush selected Norman Mineta as Secretary of Transportation. Although Muslim men between 17 and 40 years of age committed all terrorist attacks, Secretary Mineta refused to allow profiling. Does that sound like we are taking this thing seriously? This is war! For the duration, we are going to have to give up some of the civil rights to which we have become accustomed. We had better be prepared to lose some of our civil rights temporarily or we will most certainly lose all of them permanently. Additionally, do not worry that it is a slippery slope. We gave up many civil rights during WWII, immediately restored them after the victory, and in fact, added many more since then.*"[54]

Political Correctness Destroys Us. To ensure we Americans never offend anyone, particularly Isfast fanatics intent on killing us, airport security screeners no longer profile certain people. Instead, they must conduct random searches only of the following people:

- 80 year-old women,
- little kids,

---

54.   Vernon Chong, "Muslims, Terrorists, and the USA: A Different Spin on the Iraq War." Dr. Chong is a retired Air Force surgeon and past commander of Wilford Hall Medical Center in San Antonio, Texas (retired on November 1, 1994). For his bio, go to http://www.af.mil/bios/alpha.asp?alpha=C.

- airline pilots with proper identification,
- secret service agents of the President's security detail,
- 85-year old Congressmen with metal hips, and
- Medal of Honor winner and former South Dakota Governor Joe Foss.

Wake Up! However, leave alone Muslim males between the ages of 17 and 40 because profiling is discriminatory and offensive. Additionally, it is just not nice. As the writer of the award-winning story "Forrest Gump" so aptly put it, "*Stupid is as stupid does.*" Come on people; wake up! Our Country and our troops need our support and prayers.

> *Stupid is as stupid does.*

We Must Implement Profiling. We must fight and overcome the prevailing attitude by politically correct, weak-kneed secular progressives (SPs) who seek never to offend anyone. Isfast fanatics intent on killing all of us have caused airport security screeners no longer to profile certain people. That cannot stand! We must have profiling to ferret out those who intend to harm us.

Racial Profiling Now. Sun Tzu said, "*In war, practice dissimulation, and you will succeed.*"[55] Dissimulation means dissimilar or a difference. In today's warfare, it means profiling. We must differentiate or discriminate different people in our midst. *We must identify and arrest those who are out to destroy us.* We can do this effectively through racial profiling. We will succeed in the War on Terrorism if we will follow what Sun Tzu counsels us to do.

> *In war, practice dissimulation, and you will succeed.*
> **Sun Tzu**

Comprehensive, Integrated Isfast Electronic Database

Develop a comprehensive, integrated, linked, relational database management

> *We must identify and arrest those who are out to destroy us.*

---

55. Sun Tzu, *The Art of War*. Extracted on 10/15/06 from The Internet Classics Archive of the Massachusetts Institute of Technology at URL: http://classics.mit.edu/Tzu/artwar.html.

system (RDBMS) of all information on all worldwide Isfasts, terrorism, and terrorist activities.

Signals Intelligence (SIGINT)

Basically, signals intelligence (SIGINT) involves the interception of most radio, satellite, microwave, and cellular and fiber-optic communications traffic. Use SIGINT to gather current, important conversations and data on Isfasts.

Target Information

Generate target information by using Special Forces for conducting small attacks and for scouting the terrain for potential Isfast terrorist training camps and enemy bases.

Propaganda Warfare

Use massive counter-propaganda warfare against the Isfast enemy. Establish a major propaganda war against the Isfast enemy.

PR Campaign. Conduct a massive, worldwide public relations (PR) campaign to discredit Isfast terrorists. Use Voice of America (VOA), radio, television, newspapers, magazines, billboards, posters, fliers, mailers, Internet, and other media advertisements to demonize Osama bin Laden and other Isfast terrorist leaders. Do likewise with the modern-day Hitlers of Iran, Syria, and North Korea. However, *how do we demonize demons? By just reporting the truth about them.*

Disinformation

Use disinformation. Transmit disinformation to Isfast terrorists. Feed disinformation to al-Jazeera and CNN.

Counterintelligence

Take actions to counter the Isfast intelligence, espionage, and sabotage activities. Conduct covert operations to get these Isfast terrorists.

> *How do we demonize demons? By just reporting the truth about them.*

Reconnaissance

Conduct reconnaissance operations on Isfast terrorist training camps. Reconnaissance is an inspection or exploration of an area, especially one made to gather military information. When sufficient data is gathered, conduct air strikes (with bunker busters) or deploy SOFs to destroy the camp.

Chapter 9

The Enemy Within

D r. Michael Savage has written a best-selling book titled *The Enemy Within: Saving America from the Liberal Assault on Our Schools, Faith, and Military*. It is a great, best-selling book! Get it and read it. This book includes many of the reasons why we are having a difficult time winning the war on terrorism.

A talk radio sensation and *New York Times* best-selling author, Michael Savage again goes for the jugular in this latest brash, incendiary attack on the corrosive effects of liberalism on American culture. *The Enemy Within* focuses squarely on the dangers assailing the cornerstones of American life, pointing out how liberal propaganda and agendas are seeping into America's churches, schools, and even its families.[56]

Michael Savage attacks the forces of liberalism that he believes are tearing America apart. Using the same brash, abrasive style in his writing that has become a trademark of his radio show, he writes that "*the Left operates specifically to undermine God, country, family, and the military*" and that liberalism is "either treason or insanity" or "a mental disorder." He also takes on illegal immigration, the state of health care in the US, the "Hollywood Idiots," and the decline of schools and morality in general, all of which he blames on Liberals. Savage also drops bombshells such as: "*Federal courts and judges in America today are to be more feared than al-Qaida*," and Ruth Bader

> **The left operates specifically to undermine God, country, family, and the military.**
>
> **Dr. Michael Savage**
> **Author of**
> ***The Enemy Within***

---

56. Extracted from the Michael Savage website on September 11, 2006, at URL: http://www.homestead.com/prosites-prs/EnemyWithinBook.html.

Ginsberg's appointment to the Supreme Court is *"akin to appointing the general counsel of the Ku Klux Klan (KKK) to the bench."*[57]

Savage highlights blatant abuses by government, questionable suits brought by the ACLU, and morally bankrupt products coming out of Hollywood. Savage does consistently challenge readers with controversial opinions and conclusions, so it would be a shame for potential readers to dismiss his book simply on ideological grounds alone. Further, if he really gets your blood boiling, you can always call him up on his show and take him to task.[58] That is, if you have the guts to take him to task.

Treatment of AMIs in America Today

Rightfully so, the Arabs/Muslims/Islamites (AMIs) in America today are feeling the pressure from the rest of the Americans who, generally speaking, look at them with a jaundiced eye. If there is anyone who has a good understanding of religious prejudice, religious discrimination, and religious persecution, I do. As a member of the Mormon faith (The Church of Jesus Christ of Latter-day Saints), I have experienced subtle religious prejudice and discrimination throughout my life. In the early days of the church, religious persecution was open, pronounced, rampant, blatant, and despicable. However, today, religious prejudice is more subtle and, therefore, insidious, similar to racial discrimination and prejudice.

On the other hand, the AMIs in America have not experienced anything resembling the discriminations, bias, prejudice, bigotry, and persecution experience by the following groups in American history:

- ***Blacks of America***—slavery, discrimination, and being indentured servants and treated as sub-humans

- ***American of Japanese Ancestry (AJAs)***—thrown into and incarcerated in internment, detention, concentration, or relocation camps during WW II and losing all of their land, homes, and personal belongings because of "yellow fear"

---

57.   Extracted and paraphrased on 9/11/06 from a book review written by Shawn Carkonen on Amazon.com at URL: http://search.able2know.com/About/9868.html.

58.   Ibid.

- *Native Americans (American Indians)*—robbed of their lands under the guise of being bought with mere trinkets and placed in degrading Indian Reservations

- *American Chinese*—worked on building the cross-country railroads for meager wages and called "Coolies," an offensive term

- *Mormons*—persecuted, killed, had their homes burned down, lands and property stolen, and run out of Missouri under an extermination order by Governor Lilburn Boggs

AMIs have it Easy. *Relatively speaking, the AMIs in America have it easy* as did the Vietnamese, Cambodian, and other Southeast Asian (SEA) immigrants upon their mass exodus from SEA and migration to the USA following America's loss of the Vietnam War. The AJAs and American Chinese have established themselves well in the American society because they have not raised Hades, demonstrated, picketed, vandalized, and caused problems. They just ran a low profile, worked hard, acquired higher education, assimilated into society, and got involved in mainstream American society. The other Asian groups are following suit. The East Indians from India have also done quite well because they study hard, are very smart, and work hard.

> *Relatively speaking, the AMIs in America have it easy....*

Splinter Groups. Every race and/or religion have/has their smaller splinter groups that create the problems for the larger mainstream body. For example, the following mainstream groups and their problem subsets are presented here:

- *Blacks of America*—Nation of Islam (Louis Farrakhan), New Black Panther Party for Self Defense (Malik Zulu Shabazz), ACLU, and NAACP.

- *Whites of America*—American Nazi Party, Communist Party USA (CPUSA), KKK, Aryan Nation, Skinheads, White Aryan Resistance (Tom Metzger), white supremacists, John Birch Society, and left-wing/radical/SP extremists as well as right-wing/radical extremists.

- ***AMIs of America***—Isfasts (al-Qaida, Hezbollah, Hamas, Taliban), Osama bin Laden, Saddam Hussein, Mahmoud Ahmadinejad, and sleeper cells in the US.
- ***Mormons***—Ex-Mormons for Jesus (anti-Mormons), Fundamentalist LDS (polygamists), and RLDS (now called Community of Christ).

Normal Struggle for Assimilation into America. Therefore, the AMIs of America experiences much less pressure from the mainstream public than did other constituent bodies of American society. Relatively speaking, that is nothing compared to what the other aforementioned minority groups have experienced as they grew and developed in this great United States of America.

The AMIs of America can do many unheard of things that some of the earlier groups never dreamt of doing. For instance, like the present-day Blacks and Hispanics, the AMIs have been emboldened by the SPs and, hence, push back to the extent that they may overexert themselves as do the Blacks and Hispanics (including the illegal aliens). Of course, this is all part of the great American dream and process that all minority groups struggle through to become assimilated into the great American culture and society.

Dealing with American AMIs

Track Anti-Americans. Identify those AMIs in the US who celebrate, as some did, the death of nearly 3,000 innocent people and the total destruction of the World Trade Center on 9/11 and bring them swiftly to justice. If similar terrorist events occur in the US in the future, keep track of those people who are happy for our misfortunes and bring them swiftly to justice.

Deal Swiftly with Isfast Terrorists. Any AMIs caught in the act of committing terrorism in the continental United States (CONUS) should be swiftly tried and, if found guilty, should be automatically executed. Anyone caught in the act of committing terror displays *prima facie* evidence of guilt and conviction. *Lengthy, costly trials are unnecessary and counterproductive.*

Un-American and Anti-American Activities. Deport every AMI illegally residing in the US. During time of declared war, prosecute any American AMI who disrespectfully burns or defaces the American flag. Prosecute those who speak

> ***Lengthy, costly trials are unnecessary and counterproductive.***

against US policies. Prosecute those who speak against the commander-in-chief of our Armed Forces or, in other words, the President of the USA. Identify and bring to justice those who participate in un-American and anti-American activities.

Treason

Get the Enemy Within. "The Al Qaida network is not America's most dangerous enemy," Michael Savage contends in his book titled *The Savage Nation.* "*To fight only the al-Qaida enemy is to miss the terrorist network operating within our own borders. Who are these traitors? Every rotten, radical left-winger in this country, that's who.*" He may not completely agree with either major political parties, left or right, but he's absolutely convinced of one thing: *We must uphold our patriotism, strong families, and traditional American values.* Savage uses bold, biting, and hilarious straight talk to take aim

> *We must uphold our patriotism, strong families, and traditional American values.*
>
> **Michael Savage**
> **Author of**
> **The Savage Nation**

at the sacred cows of our ever-eroding culture and wages war against the "group of psychopaths" known as People for the Ethical Treatment of Animals (PETA), the ACLU, and the liberal media.[59] I like to call PETA People Eating Tasty Animals.

Savage has the Right Ideas. "*If you're tired of being attacked in school whenever you celebrate the achievements of America; if you're weary of being trampled on whenever you speak in favor of morality; if, as a Boy Scout, you've become a pariah while the perverts have become the victims, you've come to the right place.*" Savage warns that our country is losing its identity, becoming a victim of political correctness, unmonitored immigration, and socialistic ideals: "*When it comes to our culture, we're being told by liberals to let the illegal invaders as well as the legal newcomers redefine and reshape our culture into their image.*"[60]

---

59. Extracted and paraphrased on 9/11/06 from the Michael Savage website at URL: http://www.homestead.com/prosites-prs/savagenationbook.html.

60. Ibid.

Dealing with Traitors during a Declared War. *Treason should have real meaning when we are in a declared war.*

- **Wiretaps.** Wiretap those suspected of treasonous behavior, fellow travelers, pinkos (or pinko commies), violent demonstrators, destructive political vandals, the blame-America-first crowd, extremist political activists, anarchists, and anti-American misfits.

- **Arrests.** Arrest those who aid and abet the enemy during times of war (e.g., crooked politicians, extreme SP media reporters, errant judges, Hollywood elites, political activists, anti-war demonstrators, flag burners, and vandals against military property.).

> *Treason should have real meaning when we are in a declared war.*

- **Incarceration.** Incarcerate them in concentration camps (such as the one at Guantanamo) as we did to the Japanese-Americans during World War II. Japanese-Americans were incarcerated, yet they generally did not attempt to cause us to lose the war. In fact, they fought for America in the European Theater. On the other hand, the SPs in American today are fighting to cause us to lose the War on Terrorism.

- **Court Trials.** Try them in a court of law.

- **Executions.** Publicly hang or shoot them if found guilty.

Therefore, whenever we are in a period of declared war, we should prosecute for treason all those American AMIs and SPs who aid, abet, and/or comfort the militant Isfast terrorists. *Execute all guilty traitors.*

> *Execute all guilty traitors.*

A Traitor's Reward

John Walker. Remember John Walker, the modern-day Benedict Arnold? He claimed to be an American, yet he joined the extremist, radical Muslims. Yes, he joined the Taliban in Afghanistan and fought against the USA. He did that because he despised everything for which the US stands. This is similar to the "hate America" crowd.

A Common Traitor. It was only after he was injured and captured that he claimed to be an American and desired American justice, sympathy, and leniency. What a crock! What's wrong with that picture? John Walker is no more than a common traitor (even worse than Benedict Arnold) who deserves the consequences due a traitor—a public hanging.

Justice Must Be Served. Unfortunately, this traitor will receive a "politically correct" pass and will only serve a short time in prison. He should be executed as a traitor. If they put him in a military prison, he will have it made. However, if they put him in a civilian prison and let him out in the prison yard, I pity him when the other prisoners get hold of him. He may get the same justice that serial killer Jeffrey Dahmer received while in prison. Then, justice will have been somewhat served.

Remember the Economic Stimulus Bill?

Disloyal Opposition. How in the world can the president succeed or the country succeed to improve things if people of the opposite party continue to throw rocks in his path? Some people call it the loyal opposition. Anymore these days, it seems more like the disloyal opposition.

Tom Daschle. For example, I watched closely on television the discussions regarding the Economic Stimulus Bill back in President Bush's first term. The US House of Representatives quickly passed that bill. However, the minority leader of the US Senate fought it "tooth and nail." Apparently, he had his reasons (as misguided as they appeared to me) for holding up the passage of that needed bill. Yes, Tom Daschle absolutely could not put his politics aside to help our economy move ahead.

A Failure in Democrat Leadership. Daschle charged that President George W. Bush was not showing leadership in moving the economy forward. However, how in the world can George Bush do what the American people need if Daschle and his motley crew keep throwing rocks in Bush's path? Daschle should have thought more of the Country than just of his personal power and politics. Instead of accusing the President of not showing leadership, he should have

> *I wish our politicians would stop "spinning" things and do the jobs they were elected to do.*

shown leadership himself. Daschle failed to realize that when he pointed a finger at the President, he had three fingers pointing right back at himself.

Spin Meisters. Daschle said, "*It's better to pass no bill at all than to pass a bad bill.*" Just because someone declares a bill as "bad" doe not make it so. It is hard to believe that the people on the Left believe that. *I wish our politicians would stop "spinning" things and do the jobs they were elected to do.*

Received His Just Desserts. Well, Daschle and his crew were disgraceful. They failed to heed their own slogan coined by James Carville who said, "*It's the economy, stupid!*" For his actions and inaction, Daschle was rewarded by his constituency with being voted out of office. He received his just desserts. General George S. Patton said, "*Lead me, follow me, or get out of my way.*" Daschle was moved out of the way because he chose not to lead … a sad day for Daschle.

A House Divided. We need action, not just a bunch of spin and rhetoric. Rhetoric is all I seem to hear on TV anymore. All I see are politicians on television just playing politics and attempting to acquire personal gain. Now is the time for our politicians to display their leadership instead of just being cogs in the wheel. Their idiotic behavior gives much aid and comfort to the enemy … the Isfasts. Their words and actions on television enable the terrorists to fight on with greater motivation because of this political infighting. It was President Abraham Lincoln who said, "*A house divided against itself cannot stand.*"

Errant Democrat Leadership

Drumbeat of Negativism. The wildly radical Democrat Party leadership today has gone beyond the pale in fighting against our Administration, our president, our military, and our troops. Listening to this errant leadership with their daily drumbeat of negativism against everything good is depressing to say the least. *How in the world our military and our president could ever succeed if we have these traitors carrying on as they do in the middle of a major war?* How can any president or anyone else succeed with all of these supposed leaders continuously aiding and abetting the Isfast terrorists?

> *How in the world our military and our president could ever succeed if we have these traitors carrying on as they do in the middle of a major war?*

Treasonous Words and Behaviors. Sun Tzu said, *"A whole army may be robbed of its spirit; a commander-in-chief may be robbed of his presence of mind."*[61] The disloyal opposition and the errant lame-stream media do not realize it, but their treasonous words and behaviors are contributing to:

(1) prolonging the war,

(2) emboldening the Isfast terrorists to continue fighting,

(3) killing off our war fighters,

(4) affecting (negatively) the morale of our troops,

(5) polarizing our nation,

(6) destroying the unity of our citizenship, and

(7) causing our President Bush to be hated throughout the world.

Something Must Be Done. How in the world can our commander-in-chief and our military war fighters ever succeed and win if we have such a negative faction of our country continuously tearing them down at every turn? *We must do something about such traitors who spew out their venom during a time of war.* That behavior cannot and must not stand! It would not stand in China, Russia, North Korea, Iran, Syria, Cuba, or any other such countries in the world.

> *We must do something about such traitors who spew out their venom during a time of war.*

Seditious Organizations

Organizations Way Over the Line. Outlaw seditious organizations such as the following:

- Amnesty International (AI)
- American Civil Liberties Union (ACLU)
- American Communist Party or the Communist Party USA (CPUSA)
- Islamic terrorist cells
- al-Qaida

61. Sun Tzu, *The Art of War*. Extracted on 10/15/06 from The Internet Classics Archive of the Massachusetts Institute of Technology at URL: http://classics.mit.edu/Tzu/artwar.html.

- Hezbollah

- Hamas

- Remnants of the Palestine Liberation Organization (PLO)

- Council on American-Islamic Relations (CAIR)

- National Association for the Advancement of Colored People (NAACP)

- Black Panthers

- Ku Klux Klan (KKK)

- Nation of Islam (Louis Farrakhan)

- Aryan Nations (Skinheads)

- Other such subversive organizations

Put their leaders in prison. Execute those convicted in court as traitors.

NAACP on the Edge. When first formed, the NAACP served a good purpose. However, it has now outlived its usefulness. It is now a political organization, not one that helps Black people to become self-sufficient and independent, but one that keeps Black people down as slaves on the figurative plantation. Additionally, the NAACP was a very disrespectful crowd to the President of the United States, George W. Bush. The words and actions of NAACP leaders Julian Bond and Kweisi Mfume against President Bush were despicable to say the least.

Today's Politics is Morally Corrupt. When President Richard M. Nixon started out in politics, he was a good man. However, as time went on, he acquired more and more power. Historian Lord Acton (1834-1902) said, "*Power corrupts, and absolute power corrupts absolutely.*" In the end, Nixon resulted as a common crook even though on national television he said, "*I'm not a crook.*" Yeah, right!

Sad Transformations. Over the years, the NAACP has experienced an analogous transformation. Moreover, Nixon's lie is similar to the one impeached President Bill Clinton said (while glaring and pointing at us on national television), "*I never had sexual relations with that woman ... Ms. Lewinski.*" I attribute the say-

> ### *Power corrupts, and absolute power corrupts absolutely.*
>
> **Lord Acton**
> **Historian**

ing, "*Liar, liar, pants on fire*" to both Nixon and Clinton. President Teddy Roosevelt said, "*To educate a man in mind and not morals is to create a menace to society.*" With Nixon and Clinton, their families created two menaces to society.

The Media/Press

The Errant Press. Get the errant media/press to self-monitor and control themselves, or they will need to be controlled by outside forces. Today, we need more "freedom from the press" than we need "freedom of the press." *We need to apply a full-court press on the American press.*

> *We need to apply a full-court press on the American press.*

We Need Freedom from the Press. The press reports only the bad things about the United States that occur in the war zone. The press never seems to report the good things that would put us in a good light. Whose side is the press on anyway? I have my guess. That is why I believe that we need "freedom from the press."

The Lame-stream Media. Yes, it is very sad how the American media portrays our military heroes. However, what is sadder is that the majority of people out there actually believe the garbage that they are seeing, hearing, and reading from the American lame-stream media. That is the saddest thing of all.

Sucked In by CNN. Speaking from experience, I was swayed by the American media during the Vietnam Era and got so disgusted with what I saw on CNN (i.e., Communist News Network), heard on the radio, and read in the newspapers that I resigned my regular commission as a captain and exited the USAF.

Shame on Them. They can fool me once and that is shame on them; but if they fool me twice, that would be shame on me. They are not fooling me the second time over. I know what the SP media is up to this time. So, shame on them.

Get News from the Internet and Talk Radio. Hence, I do not watch ABC, CBS, NBC, and CNN, but I do watch Fox News. I do not read the *Los Angeles Times*, *New York Times*, and *Washington Post*. I get my news from the Internet and conservative talk radio (Rush Limbaugh, Sean Hannity, Bill O'Reilly, Michael Reagan, Michael Savage, Rick Roberts, and Mark Levin among others). The SP lame-stream media will not get me to hate America first, hate our military, and hate everything good for which the United States stands. However, *I see many people being sucked in by the SP media, and that is very sad indeed.*

A Failed Press. As an example, I found it interesting that no one has spoken on the radio, television, and/or written in the newspapers about the 40,000 Taliban force in Afghanistan. In the early days of the Afghan War, I remember how the radio and TV commentators said that the Taliban had over 40,000 crack troops. Remember how the Taliban called us cowards, dared us to bring our ground armies after them, and boasted how they would slaughter our troops? Well, it never happened. Did the media/press report any of that? No.

> *I see many people being sucked in by the SP media, and that is very sad indeed.*

The Press Aids the Enemy. With all of the carpet-bombing that occurred, I constantly heard from the media/press only about the many "innocent" civilians that were killed along with a few Taliban combatants. All we heard about were the several crashed US aircraft including a B-52 and so on.

The Media Never Reports Anything Bad About the Enemy. We heard on the radio and television that there were only a few thousand al-Qaida die-hards left in Kandahar and other such places. Where are the other 40,000 or so Taliban fighters? Are they hiding in caves? The media/press never reported on them.

Where is the Media on the Important News? Perhaps the B-1, B-2, and B-52 carpet-bombing runs liquidated the 40,000 Taliban troops. Perhaps our Daisy Cutters, cluster bombs, fuel-air bombs, slurry bombs, bunker busters, and Joint Direct Attack Munitions (JDAMs) turned them into mincemeat and ashes. Perhaps the AC-130 Gunships armed with those Vulcan Gatling guns cut them to ribbons. It would have been nice if the errant media/press would shed some light on the mysterious disappearance of 90 percent of the Taliban forces.

Taliban Died for Their Country. In their unusual, strange way of thinking, all of those Taliban who have passed on to join their Allah are successful in a way. As a Taliban leader once said, "*The Americans want to live, but the Taliban want to die.*" Hence, they have achieved their goal. They died for their country. Remember General George S. Patton, Jr.? He said, "*No bastard ever won a war by dying for his country.*

> *One of the biggest mistakes the Bush Administration made in these wars was to allow imbedded press reporters.*

He won it by making the other poor dumb bastard die for his country." Hence, that's what we did. We made the Taliban die for their country.

Misguided Taliban. The only very sad thing about all of this is that they (the Taliban), unfortunately, will be very surprised when they get to the other side and find that they are not going to be with Allah but will instead be in Hell with Lucifer. Very sad!

Imbedded Reporters Are a Huge Mistake. *One of the biggest mistakes the Bush Administration made in these wars was to allow imbedded press reporters.* Those sniveling rats reported only on the mistakes and bad things our military war-fighters did. They never ever reported on the bad, evil things the enemy did. What is wrong with that picture anyway? Whose side are the reporters on? No wonder Mark Twain said, "*If you don't read the newspaper, you are uninformed. If you do read the newspaper, you are misinformed.*"

The Great Senator Zell Miller Spoke the Truth. The great Senator Zell Miller said, "*For it has been said so truthfully that it is the soldier, not the reporter, who has given us the freedom of the press. It is the soldier, not the poet, who has given us freedom of speech. It is the soldier, not the agitator, who has given us freedom to protest. It is the soldier who salutes the flag, serves beneath the flag, whose coffin is draped by the flag, who gives that protester the freedom to abuse and burn that flag.*"

Unions

We should outlaw unions and strikes during wartime. Modern-day unions are dinosaurs of the past. Like the NAACP, they have outlived their usefulness. The union bosses keep the union members in bondage. They use all of their funds for paying off SP politicians willing to do their bid, i.e., getting more handouts and entitlement programs that keep their constituents on the figurative plantation.

> *We should outlaw unions and strikes during wartime.*

Political Correctness

Politically correct tools pertain to such words as appease, negotiate, diversity, compromise, communicate, peace and freedom, treaty, collateral damage, free speech, racial profiling, withdraw, cut and run, Geneva Convention, human rights, separation of church and state, civil rights, tolerance, equal rights, and free elections. *We must do away with political correctness.* It is an invention of the SPs. I prefer to be politically incorrect.

Dr. Vernon Chong, Major General, USAF, Retired, said, "*Do I blame President Bush or President Clinton before him? No, I blame us for blithely assuming we can maintain all of our political correctness, and all of our civil rights during this conflict and have a clean, lawful, honorable war. None of those words apply to war. Get them out of your head.*"[62]

> ## We must do away with political correctness.

Dr. Chong further said, "*Democracies do not have their freedoms taken away from them by some external military force. Instead, they give their freedoms away, politically correct piece by politically correct piece. Additionally, they are giving those freedoms away to those who have shown, worldwide that they abhor freedom and will not apply it to you or even to themselves, once they are in power. They have universally shown that when they have taken over, they then start brutally killing each other over who will be the few who control the masses. Will we ever stop hearing from the politically correct, about the 'peaceful Muslims'*"?[63]

Web Logs (Blogs)

Upon reading the string of messages from all the various blogs on the Internet, I come to the following conclusions:

- Either an American who is trying to be "cute" writes the inflammatory statements that start each string of messages or a misguided, not-very-bright AMI writes the inflammatory statements.

- If a "cute" American starts a thread, it only tends to generate more animosity towards AMIs. That is not a good thing.

- On the other hand, if a misguided AMI starts an inflammatory thread, it is very sad because it inflames Americans to become anti-AMI. The American AMIs must work to quell these inflammatory statements.

---

62. Vernon Chong, "Muslims, Terrorists, and the USA: A Different Spin on the Iraq War." Dr. Chong is a retired Air Force surgeon and past commander of Wilford Hall Medical Center in San Antonio, Texas (retired on November 1, 1994). For his bio, go to http://www. af.mil/bios/alpha.asp?alpha=C.

63. Ibid.

- If American Muslims desire to become a mainstream religion in the United States, they must do more to support our Country. If they do not support our Country, then it will be centuries before the majority of Americans will accept them.

These are my thoughts for improving the prevailing environment.

Anti-American Arab-Americans

I read a blog message one day from an Arab-American who was filled with vitriol against the United States. I was flabbergasted to hear a fellow American speak so anti-American. My letter of response to that man went as so:

Dear Sir:

I have read most of the public's replies to your message and found them to be at least 99 percent against what you wrote and against you in particular. I tried to read your message with a positive attitude to give you the benefit of the doubt, and I thought, perhaps, I might come to understand and agree with what you wrote. These are my conclusions:

- **Hate and Killing of the Innocent.** I agree that hate and killing innocent people are ineffective ways to create positive, constructive change … particularly change that benefits anyone.

- **AJAs Condemned Japan.** Being an American of Japanese Ancestry (AJA) myself, I absolutely do not condone or support the Japanese attack on Pearl Harbor that had occurred on December 7, 1941. After the attack on Pearl Harbor, the AJAs generally neither supported nor condoned the Japanese from Japan for that despicable act. We despised the thought that they had attacked and hurt our country … the USA.

- **AJAs Staunchly Supported the US.** In fact, we love our country (the USA) so much that all of the AJAs that joined the US Armed Forces and, as American soldiers, fought the Germans. Some of those soldiers were not even American citizens yet, but they served honorably as US Army soldiers. In fact, the greatest percentage-wise of any particular group of battlefield dead and the numbers of medals won (including the Medal of Honor) were from the AJAs of the 100th Battalion and the 442nd

Regimental Combat Team (RCT). Would you do the same and serve in the US Armed Services to fight Islamo-fascist terrorist evildoers?

- **AJAs were Most Decorated Soldiers and Units in the US Army.** These Japanese American units suffered an unprecedented casualty rate of 314 percent and received over 18,000 individual military decorations. Many were awarded posthumously for bravery and courage in the field of battle. Among the decorations received by the 100th/442nd soldiers were 1 Medal of Honor, 52 Distinguished Service Crosses, 560 Silver Stars, 28 Oak Leaf Clusters to the Silver Star, 4,000 Bronze Stars, 1,200 Oak Leaf Clusters to the Bronze Star, and perhaps most telling of the sacrifices made by these gallant soldiers, 9,486 Purple Hearts. The 442nd Combat Infantry group emerged as the most decorated combat unit of its size in the history of the United States Army. For its service in eight major campaigns in Italy and France, the 100th Battalion and 442nd RCT earned eight Presidential Unit Citations.[64]

- **Internment Camps.** Most of the AJAs back in the States were thrown into internment or detention camps (I call them concentration camps) right here in the good 'ol US of A. The politically correct term is "Relocation Centers." No other enemy nations, peoples, or religious sects were ever treated so disgracefully before, nor since, in the USA. Yet, I love this country of ours.

- **AJAs Lost Everything.** Furthermore, the incarcerated AJAs in these internment/detention camps had all of their land, property, and personal belongings confiscated by the government and never returned. To this day, the AJAs have never recovered their confiscated land, property, and personal belongings. Yet, I love this country of ours.

- **Honorable Service in the USAF.** I served honorably for over eight years in the United States Air Force and would physically fight anyone who attempts to destroy this country. This is because I love this country of ours and am very proud to be an American citizen.

- **Traitor John Walker.** Look at John Walker. He claims to be an American, yet he joined the extremist, radical Muslims and then joined

---

64. GlobalSecurity.org website, "100th Battalion, 442nd Infantry," Military Section, at the following URL: http://www.globalsecurity.org/military/agency/army/100-442in.htm.

the Taliban in Afghanistan to fight against the USA. He did that because he despises everything for which the US stands. Now, upon capture and being injured, he claims to be an American and desires American justice, sympathy, and leniency. What's wrong with that picture anyway? He is no more than a common traitor who deserves the consequences due to traitors.

- **Immigrants Should Assimilate.** New American citizens need to assimilate into the American culture and shed their old religious habits and traditions. They need to embrace the principle of freedom of religion. They need to live and let live. They need to treat women with respect, love, and understanding.

- **Do Not Be Brainwashed.** They need to educate their masses to think for themselves, not brainwash them to hate and desire to kill or be-killed to ultimately live with Allah and 72 virgins. That is fallacious thinking. Anyone who wantonly kills will neither see nor live with Allah, God, or Heavenly Father. Period! That is a fact. Period! It will never happen. The only one that wanton killers will see and live with is Satan, the Devil, or Lucifer.

Therefore, my dear sir, we cannot bring about positive change if we go around with a "chip on our shoulder." We cannot bring happiness and freedom to our people if we hate, kill, call others stupid and gullible, or try to blame others for our shortcomings and errors. We need to look inward. We need to be introspective. We need to change our-

> *When you point a finger at others, you have three fingers pointing right back at yourself.*

selves from within before we will ever change those around us. If you will do this, I know people will listen to your words with respect and may even support your positions. Until that happens, however, you are only fooling yourself.

Remember, *when you point a finger at others, you have three fingers pointing right back at yourself.* Please consider these suggestions. If you and all AMIs, and Palestinians will do these things, others will view them with honor, respect, and love. You could then become the greatest people on this earth. However, it will only happen when all of you decide to join the world community and become an integral part of the community and not attempt to dominate the world. Please consider these things.

Sincerely yours,

Your friend

Liberalism is a Mental Disorder

Michael Savage. Popular, conservative radio host Michael Savage has also joined the call to help those suffering from this devastating illness. In his new book, *Liberalism is a Mental Disorder*, Mr. Savage shares his observations of the affliction he likens to a national cancer.[65]

Top Ten Best Seller. In the book, Michael Savage chronicles what he calls the continued assault of the liberals and leftists on the "sacred pillars" of American life including marriage, the U.S. Constitution, Bill of Rights, and the Ten Commandments, in addition to a chapter on Islamo-fascism. Savage also offers readers his advice on

> *While we are thinking about the future of Mankind, all they are thinking about is their next meal and what American and/or Israeli they can kill next.*

handling the "assaults." In each chapter is a "Savage Spotlight of Truth" that purports to cast a light on how liberals spread their alleged political agenda. *Liberalism is a Mental Disorder* stayed on the Top-Ten *New York Times* best-seller list for several months after its release on April 12, 2005.[66]

---

65. John Lenin, "Movement to Classify 'Liberalism' as Mental Disorder Gains Steam," *Free Republic* website, posted on 06/04/2005 8:20:32 PM PDT. Extracted from this website on 9/11/06.

66. Extracted on 9/11/06 from Wikipedia, the free encyclopedia website, found at the following URL: http://en.wikipedia.org/wiki/Liberalism_is_a_Mental_Disorder.

Summary of Savage's Book. *This book may contain controversial issues and is biased towards the right. This overview is meant to only contain a summary of the book itself and not show the views of the editor of this page.*

1. *Savage first discusses George Bush's actions on the War in Iraq. He presents his point: if someone is going to start a war, somebody needs to end it. He suggests that with a harsh attack, our country could free Iraq and move out. Savage uses a comparison to General Patton for his plan. He concludes that with the war over, the US may have more time to focus on domestic problems.*

2. *The second chapter is about how Islamite radicals have turned Islamic religious growth into a dangerous campaign. Islam has links to most terrorist attacks that have occurred in the past 20 years. Savage goes on to reference religious passages from the Qu'ran in which it promotes the murder of non-believers. Islamo-fascists, as Savage calls radical Islamists, have become a large threat in recent years.*

3. *The author then addresses the growing problem of illegal aliens. According to estimates he received, approximately over 12-million people entered the United States illegally each year for the past several years. Even in the heightened state of alert after 9/11, all of these people are entering through the borders, most times without detection. He hypothesizes that illegal immigrants also indirectly take money from American citizens through welfare and Medicaid.*

4. *Savage then discusses lawyers. He talks about the numerous lawsuits that are brought up today that are unnecessary. One of his examples is the lawsuit of Seong Sil Kim of New York. She was given $9.9 million because she stood in front of a train to commit suicide, and the train injured her hand. Savage then points out that approximately 80 percent of doctors order unneeded tests and 74 percent refers patients to other specialists so that he or she can avoid lawsuits. Many times the tests use tax money to fund these extra tests.*

5. *Savage then discusses mass media. His example is that when Yassar Arafat died, the media glorified him as a great, progressive leader. Arafat started the Palestine Liberation Organization (PLO), which has killed millions of opposers. Arafat was indirectly responsible for millions of deaths, yet the media said he was 'innovative,' a 'freedom fighter.' He also reportedly hid*

away billions of dollars that came from different countries. The original intentions for the money were to help the impoverished people in Palestine.

6. *Savage is outraged that groups similar to and including the ACLU have caused public scenes for decades. He believes that they use old tactics, simply to make their point. His solution to this is to ignore them.*

7. *The book ends with a list of reasons why Savage believes John Kerry lost the 2004 election. Savage's biggest topic was gay marriage. He says gay marriage is opposed by too many voters who believe that only by preventing gay marriage can the institution of marriage be kept sacred. According to references, in the states that introduced a Defense of Marriage initiative on the 2004 ballot, all 11 supported the bill. Savage believes Kerry lost because too many voters could not relate to Kerry's beliefs."*[67]

SPs Do Not Consider Terrorism a Threat. Listening to a majority of the SP politicians and pundits and reading op-ed page writers, I conclude that they do not consider terrorism in the USA as a significant threat. It is more of a joke. Apparently, it has been too many decades since The Great Depression, World War II, the Korean Conflict, and the Vietnam War. People have not been exercised enough to understand the Isfast threat and peril we face. Some day, they will experience a rude awakening.

Dr. Vernon Chong, Major General, USAF, Retired, said, *"Some have gone so far in their criticism of the war and/or the Administration that it almost seems they would literally like to see us lose. I hasten to add that this is not because they are disloyal. It is because they just do not recognize what losing means. Nevertheless, that conduct gives the impression to the enemy that we are divided and weakening. It concerns our friends, and it does great damage to our cause."*[68]

The Gen X Syndrome. Generation X'ers (i.e., people born between 1965 and 1980) have really not experienced the full impact of these types of events in their lives, with the exception of 9/11, which only occurred a little over five years ago. How quickly we forget! The Gen X syndrome would explain the low

---

67. Ibid.

68. Vernon Chong, "Muslims, Terrorists, and the USA: A Different Spin on the Iraq War." Dr. Chong is a retired Air Force surgeon and past commander of Wilford Hall Medical Center in San Antonio, Texas (retired on November 1, 1994). For his bio, go to http://www.af.mil/bios/alpha.asp?alpha=C.

concern for the Isfast threat in the USA. We will wait and see what happens. When it does happen, remember, you read about it here first.

Pacifists

Show Pity and Compassion. Regarding those very few, specific AMI Isfasts who laughed at our seven astronauts tragically killed in the 2003 Space Shuttle Columbia mishap, you must remember this: *While we are thinking about the future of Mankind, all they are thinking about is their next meal and what American and/or Israeli they can kill next.* Instead of anger and hatred towards them, we must show pity and compassion for them and their distorted view of life.

Weapons. A good friend phrased it this way: Do not attack the country that invented the weapons you use, i.e., the airplane, machine gun, rifle, barbed wire, submarine, A-bomb, H-bomb, aircraft carrier, and steel-hulled ships.

More Weapons. To these, I added the following: guided bomb units (GBUs), cluster bombs, guided missiles, unmanned aerial vehicles (UAVs), intercontinental ballistic missiles (ICBMs), intermediate range ballistic missiles (IRBMs), U-2, navigation, surveillance, and communications satellites, and battle management, command, control, communications, computers, intelligence, reconnaissance, and surveillance (BMC4IRS). Additionally, I included precision-guided munitions (PGMs), daisy cutters, attack helicopters, Gattling guns, main battle tanks (MBTs), stinger missiles, sidewinder missiles, night vision, bullet-proof vests, robotics, infrared (IR) sensors, defoliation bombs, stealth bombers/fighters, napalm, airborne warning and control system (AWACS), land mines, sea mines, radar, sonar, decoys, cruise missiles, sniper scopes, M-14 rifles, and bunker busters among others. This is not to mention upcoming laser weapons, smart bullets, artificial intelligence, neutron bombs, and chemical, biological, nuclear, and radiological (CBNR) weapons. Pity and compassion follow all of the above.

More Technology. To which he retorted with the telephone, telegraph, internet, personal computer, liquid crystal display (LCD), vacuum tube, transponder, television (TV) tower, rotary bit, stealth, space transportation system (STS), global positioning system (GPS), Spam, meal, ready-to-eat (MRE), daylight bombing, television, network, microfilm, microfiche, zip files, and graphical user interface (GUI).

> *To pacifists, living under bondage is better than death.*

Warmonger or Pacifism? I would rather be accused of being a warmonger than a pacifist who would give away or surrender our country and our freedoms. The rest of us would be in bondage, while those pacifists would bow down to the enemy and do their bidding as their "hey boys." *To pacifists, living under bondage is better than death.* I totally disagree with what they want to see happen to us. I concur with Nathan Hale who said, "*I only regret that I have but one life to lose for my country.*" I also agree with Patrick Henry who said, "*I know not what course others may take, but as for me, give me liberty or give me death.*"

Pacifists Always Jump to Wrong Conclusions. A friend wrote claiming he was a pacifist. He gave his defensive reasons why I was wrong in what I had written. I wrote the following back to him:

Thank you for your thought-provoking reply. Please note, however, that I had written "those very few, specific AMIs who laughed," which do not include all AMIs. Those AMIs can probably be counted on the fingers of two hands. Thus, you, your friends, and any of the AMI people you mentioned are not included in my statement. I was referring only to those very few, specific people who laughed and reveled after the Space Shuttle Columbia disaster.

My comment has nothing to do with being anti-Arab. It has to do with those people who lack any kind of decency and respect for the dead. Those people in question showed disrespect because they hate Americans and Jews alike. I do not hate all AMIs for what they did/said. I only suggested displaying pity and compassion

> *The day we find the pacifists muzzled or dead, we will then be in deep trouble as a free country because our enemies will have overtaken us.*

(good emotions) instead of anger and hatred (bad emotions).

If you think that my message intended more than that, please accept my apologies. My intent was to make things better, not worse. Although I am neither a pacifist nor a warmonger, as a USAF veteran, I am for defending our freedoms and our way of life.

In his reply, he totally ignored responding to my response above.

Patriots will Continue to Keep Our Country Safe. By our defending our freedoms, liberty, and Bill of Rights, we also defend the rights of pacifist (as nauseating as it seems) to tear down our great country. *The day we find the pacifists muzzled or dead, we will then be in deep trouble as a free country because our enemies will have overtaken us.* Therefore, let them spout off their vitriolic accusations and poison. We patriots will quietly go on with our vigilance and in maintaining everyone's freedoms and liberty.

Sidebar. Is it not strange that picketing pacifists who profess a desire for peace often revert to violence and riots to achieve that desired peaceful condition? They are anti-war, yet they use warring tactics to achieve their ends. What's wrong with that picture anyway?"

Dissenters

Live and Let Live. I believe in the principle of "live and let live." If we keep political discussions to facts, objectivity, logic, reason, and unemotional dialogue, then we will not have any problems. As long as they do not try to kill, maim, or ruin me, we have no problems no matter how vehemently we may disagree politically.

Fight to the Death to Protect Dissenters' Rights. I may wholeheartedly disagree politically with someone, e.g., extreme secular progressives, left-wing Democrats, Hollywood, college professorial elite, pacifists, tree huggers, environmentalists (Green Peace, Sierra Club), PETA, atheists, ACLU, NAACP, unionists, communists, fascists, Nazis, socialists, Satanists, and KKK.

> *I will fight to the death to protect their rights to picket, dissent, oppose, and disagree with any of my strong core beliefs, values, philosophies, and ideologies.*

However, *I will fight to the death to protect their rights to picket, dissent, oppose, and disagree with any of my strong core beliefs, values, philosophies, and ideologies.*

Totalitarian State. If we should ever find no pickets, dissenters, and those who oppose and disagree, then it will be too late. By that time, we will be under a dictatorship, under oppression, and under a totalitarian state. A perfect example is Saddam Hussein's Iraq. In Iraq, there were no visible picketers, dissenters, and opposers of the government. What a serene country that appeared to be. That condition prevails only because it is under a dictatorship. The oppressed people live in fear. A totalitarian state prevails.

Only Peaceable Assembly Acceptable. As long as picketers, dissenters, and opposers maintain peaceful activities, I have no problems with them. However, if they get physical and start hurting people and destroying property, then, I will become a bit upset and will physically oppose them. Our Constitution gives them the right to assemble peaceably and to oppose verbally. However, it does not give them the right to kill, maim, and destroy people and property. That is where I stand on this issue.

Values Held Dear. I believe in peace through strength. I concur with what President Theodore Roosevelt said, "*Speak softly and carrying a big stick.*" I believe in being firm but fair. I believe in live and let live. I believe in being truthful, honest, faithful, and benevolent. These are some of the values I hold dear to my heart.

More on Dissenters

> *We are in a different world today. War is much quicker and more devastating.*

Mutual Respect Needed. Ours being a free country, anyone can choose to say or write what they please as well as what I write here. Everyone is entitled to his or her own opinions. I respect dissenters' opinions just as I respect our US president's opinions. I hope that dissenters and others of their ilk can display mutual respect.

Silencing Dissenters. The only thing that silenced naysayers about leaving Germany alone before both World War I and World War II started was when Germany grew very strong and actually attacked and conquered surrounding countries. This is the only way to silence dissenters. However, *we are in a different world today. War is much quicker and more devastating.* We do not have the luxury of time to play catch-up as we did in World War I and World War II.

Weapons of Mass Destruction. When nuclear mushroom clouds appear over our large cities and millions die from poison gas and deadly diseases, maybe, then and only then, will dissenters understand what President George Bush talks about regarding weapons of mass destruction (WMD).

Paradigm Shift Required. We need to "think outside of the box" and initiate a "paradigm shift" on how we view and defend against present-day totalitarian governments, dictators, and Isfasts bent on destroying the United States. Strategies such as "first strike," "offensive warfare," and "tactical nuclear attacks" may be required in certain circumstances to defend the peace and liberty of all of these dissenters so that they can continue with their vitriolic speech.

Controlling Dictators. What people do not understand is that if we did not have so many dissenters, naysayers, and those who are tearing down our country (which, to me, borders on treason), Osama bin Laden and al-Qaida would not be motivated to continue on the path they are taking. If freedom-loving countries banded together to fight these dictators and terrorists, these people would be much easier controlled, contained, and neutralized.

Dictating American Foreign Policy. In the past, all anti-war activists, pacifists, and the "blame-America-first crowd" never protect our country from attack and conquer. I, for one, will never allow weaklings like the French and previous aggressors like the Germans to dictate American foreign policy. We need to guard against those who surrender easily and those who purposefully kill innocent people. America has never been like these countries.

Display Vigilance. We need to display vigilance against those who make us weak and susceptible to the buffetings of the bullies of the world. I believe in the United States of America. I do not tear her down. I work to build her up in the face of our enemies both foreign and domestic. *The enemies from within are much more dangerous than the enemies from without.* When they destroy the proper functioning of our inner organs, there will be no way for the body to function properly.

Constitution Shall Hang by a Thread. I will fight to the death to protect their rights to picket, demonstrate, oppose, tear down, burn our flag, tell their lies, and attempt to destroy us from within. However, I will not tolerate it when they revert to violence, vandalism, and killing of

> *The enemies from within are much more dangerous than the enemies from without.*

our own to achieve their supposedly peaceful ends. The great United States of America will endure and overcome these weak cowards. *When our Constitution gets to the point of hanging by a thread, patriots vigilant and willing to fight these enemies from within shall ultimately save our Country.*

Disgraceful Retired Generals and Admirals

Defective Generals and Admirals. Sun Tzu said, "*Now the general is the bulwark of the State; if the bulwark is complete at all points; the State will be strong; if the bulwark is defective, the State will be weak.*"[69] Whether a general is on active duty or retired, he/she is a servant of the Administration and the State. In the middle of the Iraq War, 12 disgusting, disgraceful retired generals and admirals opposed the war and endorsed the loser John Kerry for president of the United States. These generals and admirals are unintelligent. That fool, John Kerry, could not fool the American electorate.

When our Constitution gets to the point of hanging by a thread, patriots vigilant and willing to fight these enemies from within shall ultimately save our Country.

Democrat National Convention. "*At … the [2004] Democratic convention … a parade of military brass [of] … 12 retired generals and admirals publicly endorsed Kerry and that night, General John M. Shalikashvili, a former chairman of the Joint Chiefs of Staff, spoke from the podium. The next night General Wesley Clark, the commander of the US attack on Yugoslavia, praised Kerry as a potential 'commander in chief.*"[70]

Weakened Our National Posture on the World Scene. *This endorsement in the middle of an ongoing war was the biggest disgraceful military*

This endorsement in the middle of an ongoing war was the biggest disgraceful military display of partisan politics that I have ever witnessed in my entire life.

69.

70.   "Democrats' War Party and the Real Way to Say NO to the Bush Agenda," *Revolutionary Worker*, 02 Aug 2004 07:15 GMT. Extracted on 10/15/06 from the Independent Media Center at URL: http://www.indymedia.org/nl/2004/08/857282.shtml.

display of partisan politics that I have ever witnessed in my entire life. To say the least, I was appalled! When on active duty, generals and admirals should follow orders and support their commander-in-chief ... or resign if they cannot support the national policy. After they retire, they should keep their mouths shut and stay out of politics or actively run for political office. These retired generals and admirals comprise a bunch of jokers who weakened our national posture on the world scene.

Worst President in History?

> ### We didn't start the war on terror. Try to remember. Terrorists started it on 9/11.

We Did Not Start the War on Terror. *"Some claim President Bush shouldn't have started this [the Iraq] war. They complain about his prosecution of it. One person recently claimed Bush was the worst president in U.S. history. Let's clear up one point: We didn't start the war on terror. Try to remember. Terrorists started it on 9/11. Let's look at the 'worst' president and mismanagement claims:*

- *FDR led us into World War II. Germany never attacked us: Japan did. From 1941-1945, 450,000 lives were lost; an average of 112,500 per year.*

- *Truman finished that war and started one in Korea. North Korea never attacked us. From 1950-1953, 55,000 lives were lost; an average of 18,333 per year.*

- *John F. Kennedy started the Vietnam conflict in 1962. Vietnam never attacked us.*

- *Johnson turned Vietnam into a quagmire. From 1965-1975, 58,000 lives were lost; an average of 5,800 per year.*

- *Clinton went to war in Bosnia without UN or French consent. Bosnia never attacked us. Sudan offered Osama bin Laden's head on a platter to Clinton three times, and he did nothing. Osama has attacked us on multiple occasions.*

- *In the two years since terrorists attacked us, President Bush has liberated two countries, crushed the Taliban, and crippled al-Qaida. He put nuclear inspectors in Libya, Iran, and North Korea without firing a shot and captured a terrorist [Saddam Hussein] who slaughtered 300,000+ of his own people.*

- *We lost 600 soldiers, an average of 300 a year. Bush did all this abroad while not allowing another terrorist attack at home.*

Worst president in history? The facts do not support that assertion. Come on!"[71]

Students. We need to do extensive background checks on all foreign AMI students in the United States taking pilot training, courses in nuclear physics, and military science training. Put "tails" on suspicious AMI students. Indeed, we should stalk them (as a stalker does) every day at all hours of the day and night.

Can We Lose the War on Terrorism?

Dr. Vernon Chong, Major General, USAF, Retired, said, *"Again, the answer is simple. We can lose the war by 'imploding.' That is, defeating ourselves by refusing to recognize the enemy and their purpose, and really digging in and [not] lending full support to the war effort. If we are united, there is no way that we can lose. If we continue to be divided, there is no way that we can win!"*[72]

---

71.   Blog item posted on 04/20/2004 7:41:41 PM PDT by an Afghan-Iraq Veteran. Extracted on 9/14/06 from the Free Republic Website located at URL http://www.freerepublic. com/focus/f-news/1121506/posts.

72.   Vernon Chong, "Muslims, Terrorists, and the USA: A Different Spin on the Iraq War." Dr. Chong is a retired Air Force surgeon and past commander of Wilford Hall Medical Center in San Antonio, Texas (retired on November 1, 1994). For his bio, go to http://www. af.mil/bios/alpha.asp?alpha=C.

Chapter 10

Conversations with a Liberal

A very liberal friend of mind and I held discussions regarding Islamo-fascists (Isfasts) and the War on Terrorism. He and I disagree on just about everything political. We are friends because we do maintain common ground in engineering, management, and family values. The discussion centered on some of the following topics. Here goes.

Debating Rules of Engagement

Fact-gathering Mission. Please forgive me if my responses irritate, aggravate, and/or upset you. I am on a fact-gathering mission to solicit thoughts from a genius extremist liberal mind. All of this is good fodder for my book. I may come across pretty blunt in my responses, which may shock you sometimes. However, I just want to get your true feelings no matter how distorted I may feel they may be or how emotional they may appear. So, if you do not mind, bear with me and not take anything personal.

Value of Listening to Ultra-Liberal SPs. Keep your ideas coming! I need to hear the extremist views of the left wing, radical, extremist, ultra-liberal secular progressives (SPs) in this country so that I can formulate ways to counter their arguments.

Seeking the Truth. *Sometimes we suffer from scotomas or blind spots.* Sometimes we suffer from groupthink and follow a particular political party's talking points, which I notice a lot of partisan people expound. Sometimes we need a paradigm shift to see things differently. All I want to do is to get as close to the truth as possible, and I can only do that by listening to all viewpoints. If you do likewise, we can continue to have meaningful dialogue.

> *Sometimes we suffer from scotomas or blind spots.*

Viable Sources must Support All Assertions. *Liberal's Comment—The Shah allowed Mobil Oil and other oil companies to take over the oilfields that were* *going to be nationalized by the democratically elected government of Iran in 1953. The companies then started robbing the people of Iran of their God-given natural resource, selling it, and making a profit. THAT is stealing, immoral in my book.* **Uda's Response**—This is not true. If you believe it to be true, please provide documented proof by directing me to a URL on the Internet that verifies your assertion. Make sure the source is an objective, impartial source with no axe to grind. Sending me to a biased source does not prove your point. Thank you. [He never responded to this request indicating its untruth.]

Rose-color Lenses. *Liberal's Comment*—*I am merely speaking the truth as I see it.* **Uda's Response**—Be introspective. I fully realize that you believe you are speaking the truth as you see it. However, realize that you may be looking through rose-color lenses. What you think you see may not necessarily be the truth. Then, you believe it to be the truth because that is what you know. This is why I solicit your opinions and how you see things. Just in case I am seeing things through rose-color lenses, I want to make the necessary adjustments to my view of things.

Selective Listening/Reading. *Liberal's Comment*—The *term Islamo-fascist is found to be insulting and offensive by Muslims. That's just like referring to the Northern Ireland Catholics, even those who don't commit violence, as "Catholic Fascists." That may offend all Catholics. It's a religious baiting term. I assure you that most of the Muslims in the world are not like that. Really nice people.* **Uda's Response**—Nobody is confusing religious extremists with all Iranian people. How you leap to this conclusion is beyond me. Never have I ever insinuated what you are saying here. It appears that you are exercising selective listening/reading. Please do not twist my words around and make it sound like I am against all Iranians. You obviously did not read what I wrote. Please go back and re-read what I wrote about it. To refresh your memory, here is what I wrote:

"If I used the terms Arab-fascists, Muslim-fascists, or Islamic-fascists, someone will be insulted/offended. That is not the point. If one does not commit violence, one should not feel offended by the use of the term. I define the term "Islamo-fascists" as extremist, radical, fundamental Islamists, i.e., those who have hijacked the Islamic religion. They are the ones who are brainwashing their children into becoming suicide bombers. It does not mean anything else than that. Those who get offended are usually the supporters of these radical folks, which are not few in number. More than 100-million folks comprise this radical group of people. A former terrorist on television said this number could be up to 150-million people."

Emotional Outbursts. *Liberal's Comment—Bob, you haven't answered my question, just another emotional outburst.* **Uda's Response**—I have answered your question. Just because you disagree with my answer does not mean that it is "just another emotional outburst." Just calling something an emotional outburst does not make it so. I can turn around and call your statement an emotional outburst myself. However, I will not do that because I want to hear your explanations even though I may disagree with them. Further, just because I disagree with them, does not make them emotional outbursts. So, please refrain from name-calling, finger pointing, and emotionalism (not outbursts, just emotionalism).

Logic is Irrefutable. *Liberal's Comment—See logical reason above to refute emotional outburst.* **Uda's Response**—I have not seen logical reasoning yet coming from what you wrote … only emotional outburst. Two can throw rocks. I want logical reasoning (not by your claim only) but words that I agree as being logical. *One person's logic is another person's illogic.* If an argument is logical, both parties should agree that it is logical. Logic is irrefutable. If I refute any explanation you give, you have not provided me with logical reasoning. For something you say or write to be logical, I must agree that it is logical. If not, all you have given me are opinions, thoughts, personal philosophy, personal beliefs, and emotional outbursts.

> *One person's logic is another person's illogic.*

Eyes Wide Open. Trust me. I have both of my eyes wide open. I know exactly what I see and proceed with objectivity and logic. As you see things through your own special lenses, I am sure you do likewise.

Agree to Disagree. *Liberal's Comment—Phew, Bob! I thought you'd tell me to go to Hell! Actually, I don't believe in Hell. This is Hell.* **Uda's Response**—I would not tell you to go to Hades. You are too good of a friend and source of liberal thinking. At least I am willing to hear your wild ideas, even though I may disagree with most of them. I hope we are both mature enough to agree to disagree and not get personal about it and become disagreeable.

Read the Book. *Liberal's Comment—How far have you gotten with selling it to the President? Have the newspapers pounced on it? If not, what good is it?* **Uda's Response**—You must strive not to be insulting and refrain from personal attacks. All good things take time. I am working to get the Administration to change their approach in all future

> *We should never go to war unless attacked.*

battles/wars. *We should never go to war unless attacked.* When we do go to war, we should go to war to win. Never take the war of attrition approach. Wars should be short to minimize the loss of lives by getting the perpetrators of wars. Enough said. Read the book.

Dealing with the Enemy

There are Alternatives. *Liberal's Comment—Who killed the electric car? Detroit.* **Uda's Response**—That may be true up to now, but when push comes to shove, the oil lobby will give way to another way of obtaining our needed energy. There are alternatives. We are currently making big efforts to find these oil alternatives. We will find viable alternatives. When we do, we will leave the Middle East in the cold, and only Russia, China, North Korea, Venezuela, Cuba, Iran, Syria, and other such totalitarian countries will buy Middle East oil. When we find good alternatives, we will not need Middle East oil. Thank goodness!

The Hitler of Iran. *Liberal's Comment—How can he [i.e., Ahmadinejad] be Hitler? He did not kill the Jews or take over Europe. By the way, the latter was a good thing. It weakened the Colonial powers forcing them to give up their colonies.* **Uda's Response**—You must agree either that the Holocaust did not occur as the Iranian Hitler, Mahmoud Ahmadinejad, so stated or that the German Hitler actually did slaughter six-million Jews. You cannot play two ends against the middle. Ahmadinejad is an Iranian Hitler because he is walking the same path that the original German Hitler walked. He plans to kill millions of people of the West, i.e., us, with nuclear weapons that he is currently developing. I come to the feeling that you either do not believe that his goal is to kill all of us or you sympathize with him as you had previously stated that you agree with "the president of Iran."

Ahmidinejad No Hitler? Thank you for the attached story on regarding your subject: "Ahmadinejad is no Hitler."[73] I enjoy the statements below regarding:

- *"Ahmadinejad is no Hitler"*

---

73.   Ray Takeyh, "Ahmadinejad is No Hitler," *Los Angeles Times*, latimes.com opinion article, November 19, 2006. Extracted on 11/24/06 from http://www.latimes.com/news/opinion/la-op-takeyh19nov19,0,7659757,story?coll=la-opinion-rightrail. Takeyh is a senior fellow at the Council on Foreign Relations and the author of *Hidden Iran: Paradox and Power in the Islamic Republic.*

- *"The world's most rash leaders can be contained, and the nuclear-ambitious Iranian president is no exception."*

- *"If you think Iranian President Mahmoud Ahmadinejad makes outlandish comments, consider what Mao Tse-tung said to a visiting head of state in 1954: 'If someone else can drop an atomic bomb, then I can too. The death of 10 or 20 million people is nothing to be afraid of.'"*

Uda's Response—Please understand that this article is an "opinion" piece. These thoughts are only Ray Takeyh's opinions. *Opinions are not facts.* So, please do not present such outlandish opinions as facts. *You cannot win an argument using opinions.*

> **Opinions are not facts.**

Additionally, the interesting thing is that Mao Tse-tung receives credit for killing 38 million people during his reign of terror and during the Cultural Revolution. We have nothing to fear because Mao killed mainly Red Chinese people.

> **You cannot win an argument using opinions.**

Only one slight difference between Mao and Ahmadinejad is that the Iranian Hitler vows to kill all Americans and infidels in the world. That'll be only a few hundred million people up to about maybe 1 billion Western people in the world. That will leave at least 5 billion Chinese, Indians, and AMIs in the world. It should be a much better world with those people left over without any Europeans and Americans (So I am not misquoted, I am being sarcastic here.).

Sorry, I just see it from a different perspective. However, I do hope you and all liberals are correct in your assessment of the Iranian president. Remember, General Karl von Clausewitz, the great Prussian general and military strategist, said, *"The conqueror is always a lover of peace; he would prefer to take over our country unopposed."*[74]

The Great Satan. *Liberal's Comment—They don't say they blame the US for all of their problems. Where did you hear that?* **Uda's Response**—I heard it from Noni Darwish, an American Iranian whose father was killed by his own people (he was a martyr). She and others on a television special stated that the extremist

---

74. Karl von Clausewitz, *On War*. Extracted on 12/10/06 from http://www.military-quotes. com/Clausewitz.htm.

Islamists blame all of their own problems on the US, which they consider as The Great Satan. I assume you believe that the US is The Great Satan also. Right or wrong?

We Defend Ourselves, Not Police the World. *Liberal's Comment—So go ahead and defend the country: build stronger borders, etc. How can going over to someone else's country and killing their inhabitants constitute defending our country? When you want to be the self-appointed policeman of the world, expect to be kicked in the shins when you piss people off.* **Uda's Response**—We are not self-appointed policemen of the world.

> # We are not self-appointed policemen of the world.

You seem to have a very short memory, which is typical of liberals. Have you forgotten what happened on September 11, 2001? Remember, al-Qaida attacked the USA when they leveled the Twin Towers, crashed a plane into the Pentagon, and crashed another plane in a Pennsylvania field killing all toll of about 3,000 innocent people. If I recollect correctly, we were attacked. We defended ourselves by attacking the Taliban and al-Qaida in Afghanistan and Iraq who supported Hamas human suicide bombers, the Taliban, and al-Qaida. The next will be Iran, who supports Hezbolla, Hamas, and al-Qaida.

Random Thoughts. *Liberal's Comment—Israel should be moved out of the Muslim neighborhood. I agree with the president of Iran. Why should the Palestinians have to suffer because Hitler killed the Jews. They need to get their land back. Anyways, I don't have the mind to get involved with it because the Chinese Communists have threatened India. They prey on those they consider weak—Chinese expansionism—they're restating their claim to large amounts of Indian land.* **Uda's Response**—The Israelis have a right to be there. The Muslims should just live and let live. You agree with that Hitler! *According to the Hitler of Iran, Adolph Hitler didn't kill any Jews. He said that the Holocaust did not happen.* Hence, you either have to accept one or accept the other. You cannot play two ends against the middle. That's not playing fair.

Yes, the Palestinians do not need to suffer because the German Hitler killed the Jews. However, the Palestinians are killing many innocent civilians through their suicide bombers. The Israelis are only defending themselves against these homicidal killers. That is what the Palestinians need to suffer for, not because Hitler killed the Jews.

The Palestinians need to get their land back? So do the American Indians (or Native Americans for you who want to be politically correct), the Hawaiians, the Mexicans, the Russians, and the Chinese. Hey, you lose the land, that's tough luck. What about all the land and property the US confiscated from the American-Japanese when they threw them into detention camps during WWII? Should they not get their land back too? It's just too bad!

> ***According to the Hitler of Iran, Adolph Hitler didn't kill any Jews. He said that the Holocaust did not happen.***

What do you care about the Chinese Communists threatening India? Aren't you an American citizen now? It's like me caring about the welfare of Japan just because I am a Japanese person by racial extraction. Who cares? It's their problem.

Land Ownership. *Liberal's Comment—The Palestinians were there first. They have a right to that land, not Europeans set up by the US. Look at South Africa, Zimbabwe, Angola, and Algeria. The white man got booted out of there. He killed a lot of people and when the going got rough, he ran away. Same thing will happen in Palestine. Oh, by the way, Ronald Reagan supported the white regime in South Africa and was against one-man rule. Shame on him.* **Uda's Response**—Regarding your comment that Palestinians were there first, it does not matter. As I had pointed out, many people were there first. If they lost the land by hook or crook, that is just too bad. If you want to get to who really owned the land, the cave men originally owned the land. Hence, the land rightfully belongs to them and not to all of those people you listed.

> ***All the land on earth belongs to Adam and Eve.***

Furthermore, if you were a Christian, Adam and Eve really were here first (even before the cave men). Therefore, *all the land on earth belongs to Adam and Eve.* So, can you see how ridiculous your arguments are regarding who owned the land first?

Moving the Jews. *Liberal's Comment—I'm just trying to avoid the killing by moving Israel to Australia, Texas, or Nevada.* **Uda's Response**—You state in passing that we can move the Israelis to Australia, Texas, or Nevada. Obviously, you do not really care who currently owns the land. You want to move the Israelis anywhere of your choosing? It is no different than the decision that was made to move the Jews to Palestine after WWII.

You need to make more sense of your arguments. You cannot argue against an approach previously taken to move the Jews after WWII and call it unfair. Then, turn right around and use that same apparently unfair approach to move the Israelis somewhere else today. You cannot rightfully do that without any fairness given to those who currently own the land!

More Liberal Ramblings. *Liberal's Comment—The Iranians have a right to nuclear power and the right to defend their country with a nuke. The US went there in 1955 and toppled their democratic government setting up the Shah of Iran. Then they stole their oil. When the Shah got toppled, they held US hostages. Why? Why not Canadian hostages? Because they had a beef with America. Then the US, France, Great Britain, and Germany gave chemical weapons to Saddam Hussein, which he used on them. Therefore, they have a right to defend their country. They say "Never again." I don't blame them. When oil becomes scarce, the US will go taking over weak countries. Iran wants to be prepared.* **Uda's Response**—If they were decent, civilized people, it would be more palatable. However, their goal is to dominate the world and have a one-world religion … radical, fundamentalist Islamism. That cannot stand.

True, the US set up the Shah, but it is false that we stole their oil. The US paid big bucks for the oil, just as we are doing so today. Stealing means we get it free. Nothing is free. We pay for all of that filthy oil. *The Iranians have a beef with America because they're just jealous.*

> **The Iranians have a beef with America because they're just jealous.**

Yes, Iran has a right to defend itself, just as we have a right to defend our country. They say don't blame them for anything. They say the US is at fault for everything that goes wrong in Iran. Something is wrong with that kind of mindset.

No, we will not take over weak countries. Instead, we will eventually develop an alternative source of energy for running our automobiles. Then, we won't be buying any Mid-Eastern oil. However, watch out, they'll blame us for racism and not buying their oil. That's when I'll laugh in their faces. Yes, they want to be prepared for WW III, Armageddon, and Doom's Day. They will get what they are working towards.

Iran will Nuke Israel. *Liberal's Comment—Anyways, leveling the Sunni Triangle will kill many innocent people. It will also hand over the country to the Shias who have more in common with Iran. Do you want that? That's what that Prime Minister over there is doing, using the US to strengthen the Shias hands. Remember he doesn't want the US to go into Shia areas to even search for missing people.* **Uda's Response**—It is okay that the Shiites have more in common with Iran. The Hitler of Iran will drop a nuke on Israel. Then, we (the US) will be in there to level Tehran, Iran. We will take over and implement another Marshall Plan. Eventually, we will turn the country over to the more moderate Shiites to run that country under more civilized rule.

We would give the innocent civilians a chance to exodus in 48 or 72 hours. However, you must remember, the al-Qaida terrorists use innocent civilians as human shields. Hence, they put those innocent civilians at risk in harms way. At least carpet-bombing of the Sunni Triangle is something to consider and think about.

You and Murtha have no real idea of what the US military can do if these brainless politicians would let the military generals fight the war to win. We could easily handle Iran, Syria, and North Korea simultaneously if the politicians would unleash our tactical nuclear weapons. A tactical nuclear war would not be as bad as most people believe. It would solve problems quickly with far less people killed and/or wounded.

Our military has its hands tied behind its back and expected to fight a war of attrition run by our incompetent politicians. That is no way to fight a war. We should never go to war except to win quickly. Additionally, we win quickly by using all of the resources at our disposal to accomplish that end.

> *We should never go to war except to win quickly.*

The A-bombing of Hiroshima and Nagasaki killed many, many innocent people. However, dropping two A-bombs ended WWII quickly, which saved at least 2-million military personnel on both sides. Hence, killing a few thousand innocent civilians through collateral damage may be the better alternative.

Even More Liberal Ramblings. *Liberal's Comment—Nuking people is not the answer, except for the Chinese Communist government of course! As a religious per-*

son, I'm still surprised that you cling to this point of view. Whatever happened to your 10 Commandments? You need to come up with a clear plan for Iraq. In the absence of a clear plan, what's the sense in our troops getting killed? **Uda's Response**—Nuking Japan was the answer to ending WWII. It would be nice, clean, and easy solution for the Iran problem.

Nowhere in the 10 Commandments that says we should be "pacifists." Nowhere in it that says we cannot defend ourselves especially against an enemy that wants to kill all of us for Allah's sake. Nowhere in the 10 Commandments that says we cannot hit our enemies with nuke weapons. So, what's the beef? Rolling over and giving up is not part of the 10 Commandments. Please don't play the 10 Commandments card on me. That's playing unfair.

I have a clear plan for Iraq. Read my book when it comes out. You may not have the stomach to accept the plan. It is a plan for winning, not losing as we have right now.

Our troops are there on their own volition. If they were not there risking their lives, you would not be able to spout out all of that venom that you do. They are protecting your right to tear down the Administration and badmouth all for which this country stands.

If our troops want out, they can get out any time they decide. They call it desertion. The other way is to resign. Another way is not to re-enlist. Moreover, another way is to retire. They are not forced against their will to be there.

If I were a young man, I would volunteer to be there to protect your right to tear down everything for which we stand. As I had said before, I will defend your right to the death to be as opposing and cantankerous as you so desire.

> *I have a clear plan for Iraq. Read my book when it comes out. You may not have the stomach to accept the plan. It is a plan for winning, not losing as we have right now.*

Dealing with the Problem at Home

Ethnic Neighborhoods in the US. *Liberal's Comment*—*That's where my roots are, my culture, my heritage, my background. You go to an Italian, Irish,*

Mexican, Korean, Chinese, etc. neighborhood, you get the same thing there. There is nothing wrong with it. **Uda's Response**—Yes, there is nothing wrong with it as long as you do not get your loyalties as an American vs. your former country mixed up. If you feel more loyalty to your motherland, then perhaps you should return to your motherland (please do not get emotional about this and retaliate with personal epithets).

I am serious. If I had a stronger affinity for Japan over the United States, I would move to Japan and become a Japanese citizen. However, I am an American and shall defend the United States over any others in the world. Simmer down. Do not get your bowels in an uproar. Your true allegiance reveals itself depending on how upset you get with my suggestion. I am just being pragmatic here.

Neo-Conservative (Neocon)? *Liberal's Comment*—*If you open you eyes, I can deal with you, but for the same old Neocon thinking, I can't!* **Uda's Response**—What is your definition of a Neocon? I would like to know exactly what you mean by that term. If I think I understand the term, I do not believe that I am a Neocon. I think I am more of an Old-fashion Conservative (Ofcon). The *Merriam-Webster Online Dictionary* defines "neocon" as *a former liberal espousing political conservatism*. The Neocons are more like right-wing liberals and right-wing democrats. That is definitely not "my cup of tea."

After the Democrats Take Over. If you really believe the Democrats can do a better job than Bush is doing, then you should get Hillary Clinton, John Kerry, or Al Gore elected president in 2008. Then we will really see how bad things can get. I cannot wait to see the chaos that will result after the Democrats start running the country again in 2007. *Be ready for combat in California.*

> *Be ready for combat in California.*

New Speaker of the House Starts Out on Wrong Foot. *Liberal's Comment*—*How to beat them is to withdraw from Iraq. Like Murtha said, bring the troops home to Okinawa. That should do it. The reason for them to be in Iraq will have disappeared. Look what happened in Vietnam. All those dire predictions and likely consequences didn't materialize. This is: all those people died for nothing. Same thing in Iraq. No plan, just likely consequences preying on 9/11 extended fears. Come home and strengthen the borders.* **Uda's Response**—Evidently the Democrats did not like Congressman Murtha (or his mantra of pulling out of Iraq now) as they rejected him for the more moderate Steny Hoyer. Nancy Pelosi lost political leverage when she strongly backed Murtha on that poor choice.

What we should do is to level the Sunni Triangle, and then get out of Iraq. That would get rid of a whole lot of the Isfasts. The Murtha-ish idea of getting out of Iraq will rid Iraq of Isfasts is flawed. The Isfasts will then be fighting us in Los Angeles, New York, San Francisco, Chicago, Houston, San Diego, and other major American cities. I would rather wipe them out in Iraq than in San Marcos, California, or Los Angeles, California.

Murtha is Worn Out. *Liberal's Comment*—As *Murtha said, the US military is worn out—it needs rest and to be rebuilt.* **Uda's Response**—Congressman Jack Murtha falsely claimed that our military is worn out. That is not true. Instead, Jack Murtha is worn-out. Remember, he just lost the election to become the majority leader of the House of Representatives. That result is good for our country because Jack Murtha is one of the worst congressmen in the US House of Representatives.

> *Jack Murtha is one of the worst congressmen in the US House of Representatives.*

President Bush—Gargantuan Disappointment. *Liberal's Comment*—My *point is that there is no clear plan right now. Spell out a clear plan with an exit strategy. President Bush has none and neither does anybody [else].* **Uda's Response**—President Bush has been a huge disappointment to us grass-roots conservatives. Of course, Bush is a left-leaning Republican who is a Globalist at heart, which is sad. He has totally botched the sealing of the US-Mexican border.

> *President Bush has been a huge disappointment to us grass-roots conservatives.*

John McCain's Liberal Tendencies. *Liberal's Comment*—Even McCain who *advocates more troops in Iraq was asked if his idea would work. He replied he didn't know. Try this, try that. In the mean time innocent people are being killed and we're losing the best of our youth.* **Uda's Response**—John McCain is not a very good candidate to become President of the US. He has too many liberal tendencies (no offense to you intended). I like you as a human being and as a person even though I totally disagree with your politics and ideology. That is okay. As long as we have mutual respect, I am sure we can both live together in peace.

Chapter 11

The UN—A Worthless Organization

The United Nations (UN) is a useless, worthless organization characterized by the following negatives:

- **Waste of Money.** A waste of our taxpayers' money. Why do we pay good money to fund an illegal, immoral, unethical organization used by rogue nations for political and financial gain?

- **Anti-American.** An anti-American organization. So, why do we fund it?

- **Filthy Organization.** A crooked organization filled with criminals, spies, murderers, thieves, liars, and cheaters. When are we going to wise up and withdraw from the UN?

- **Graft and Scandal Ridden.** Graft and scandal infested. For example, look at the "Food for Oil" scandal. Also called the "Oil for Food" scandal. It all depends on your frame of reference. "Graft" is the acquisition of money, position by dishonest or unjust means, as by actual theft or by taking advantage of a public office or any position of trust or employment to obtain fees, perquisites, profits on contracts, legislation, and pay for work not done or service not performed; illegal or unfair practice for profit or personal advantage.[75]

> *The United Nations (UN) is a useless, worthless organization.*

- **Only a Debate Club.** The UN is a useless, time-wasting debate club. All that rhetoric ends in written, watered-down proclamations, resolutions, and laws that no rogue or pariah nation follows, obeys, or respects. What a waste of time, energy, and money! Endless talk solves nothing.

---

75. The definition of "graft" was extracted on 9/2/06 from the *Brainy Dictionary* found at the following URL: http://www.brainydictionary.com/words/gr/graft170152.html.

I participated in the Model United Nations (MUN) in college. It was fun at the time. However, looking back on it, I conclude that it was nothing but a huge waste of time. *Mad* Magazine's Alfred E. Neuman said, "*The UN is a place where governments opposed to free speech demand to be heard!*"[76] What is wrong with that picture anyway?

- **Propaganda Machine for Tyrants.** The UN is a propaganda machine for tyrants. Unstable Marxist/fascist tyrants like Iranian President Mahmoud Ahmadinejad and Venezuelan President Hugo Chavez grandstand in general assembly sessions of the UN just for worldwide propaganda purposes and to denigrate the US. Why do we allow low-life animals like these to come to our country and lambaste us the way they did in September 2006?

  > "*The UN is a place where governments opposed to free speech demand to be heard.*"
  >
  > **Alfred E. Neuman**
  > *Mad Magazine*

  We should not allow them to set foot on our soil. If they do not like it, then they can pay to move the UN building to Iran, Venezuela, Russia, China, North Korea, Syria, Cuba, or any other such totalitarian country. Let them bear the burden of the wasteful UN.

- **Meaningless Legislation Generator.** The UN is a political animal that passes meaningless proclamations, resolutions, and laws that crooked, unethical countries ignore. What a waste!

  It seems that the people who like the UN are mainly Democrats and secular progressives. I believe it is because it furthers their two primary motivations, i.e., power and money. The Democrats are mainly out for power, position, and dominance. Along with that, if any of them get rich quickly, just "follow the money trail." Money and power ... that's it!

---

76.   Quote extracted on 10/7/06 from "Alfred E. Neuman Quotes" at URL http://www.leedberg.com/mad/quotes/quotes.html.

Many Republicans are no different than Democrats. Money and power …
that's it! In addition, somewhere in there, they (both parties) seem to be able to fit in their secondary motivators, i.e., booze and sex. Yes, money, power, booze, and sex. Those are their motivators

> ### Many Republicans are no different than Democrats.

that make them strive for lifelong careers in politics. Politics in the UN is just an extension of our US national politics. It's all so disgusting.

- **Hampers the US.** The UN is an organization established mainly to tie the US's hands. We follow the rules. We keep ethically in line. We pay our dues. What do we get in return? Screwed, that's what! Are we gluttons for punishment? Why do we continually subject ourselves to this negative gas?

- **Neither Stops Wars nor Creates Peace.** The UN cannot and does not stop any wars. Wars and the problems of the world keep going on. There is never any period of peace. General George S. Patton was correct when he said, *"Perpetual peace is a futile dream."* So, why are we wasting our time, energy, and money playing in the UN sandbox?

- **Diplomacy.** No diplomacy goes on at the UN. Where is it, anyway? Why is Ex-president Clinton hanging around the UN politicking, anyway? I believe he is campaigning to become the next Secretary-General of the UN … yes, President of the World! His ego never ceases and desists. *Bill Clinton wants to become President of the World.* Unbelievable!

- **Cadre of Criminals.** UN diplomats disobey and ignore our laws. They are immune to paying any parking and traffic fines. They are immune to prosecution for rape and other heinous crimes. They call it diplomatic immunity. What a crock!

Those diplomats commit espionage, rape, theft, and other federal crimes, yet the worst punishment that these criminals can receive is deportation. Then, the next criminal is sent to the US to replace the deported criminal. Disgusting! There are many

> ### Bill Clinton wants to become President of the World.

more disadvantages than advantages to retaining the UN on American soil. We should get rid of the UN!

Eliminate the UN

If the UN constantly works against us, we should then:

- Abandon and withdraw from the UN.

- Stop paying our dues to the UN.

- Ignore any UN resolutions written against us just as our enemies (Iran, North Korea, Syria, and formerly Iraq) reject them.

- Go it alone but with the aid and support of our "true" allies (e.g., England, Canada, Australia, Japan, South Korea, Philippines, and Italy) against the Axis of Evil. Be very leery of France, Germany, Spain, Russia, China, Saudi Arabia, Egypt, and other such undependable countries.

- Kick the UN out of New York.

- Stop giving financial, military, and other resource aid to the many fence-sitting countries (called mugwumps) on which we are wasting our tax dollars.

Withdraw Funding

If any country that receives money from the United States proves to be anti-American, we should immediately pull the American taxpayer funds that flow into that country. Why do we support those who are against us? We should be pouring dollars into the few countries that support us. How ignorant can our politicians be?

The more money we give to nations that hate us, they hate us even more. Additionally, they think (actually know) we are dumb for giving money that they use to purchase weapons to fight against us. It does not take a genius or rocket scientist to know what countries we should not support financially. Our politicians who support wasting our money that way are either moronic or dumb. Take your pick.

> *The more money we give to nations that hate us, they hate us even more.*

Chapter 12

Uncontrolled Illegal Immigration

The illegal alien problem is President George W. Bush's biggest failing in his presidency and Administration. *There appears to be no political will by both parties to resolve this problem.* It is all because both parties want the votes of illegal aliens. How silly is that? Our errant politicians care more about power and votes than they do about sustaining the law, the well-being of the country, and doing what is right. Sickening!

Immigrants, Not Americans, Must Adapt

Immigrants Should Become Americans in Deed. People who immigrate to the United States should do it legally, go through proper channels, wait their turn, and become true Americans when they receive their citizenship. They should learn to speak the national language, which is American English. Immigrants should assimilate into the communities throughout the United States. They should not cluster in little strongholds that breed mistrust, separatism,

> *There appears to be no political will by both parties to resolve this problem.*

and continued loyalties to their previous native lands. When people become Americans, they should cast off their allegiance to their former countries.

No Misplaced Loyalties. Immigrants should assimilate into the American culture, not push their culture upon the existing American society. They should be loyal to this country, not to the one they left. If not, why come to the United States in the first place? Being here just for the benefits is totally unacceptable. *With citizenship comes responsibility.* Every citizen is expected to build this country, to protect this country, and to obey its laws.

Support Our Country. Citizens of the United States should believe in and practice "freedom of religion," not force their "fundamentalism" upon us. Peaceful persuasion is one thing, but coercion is totally another matter. They should support our country, not tear it down. It is very sad that the SPs of our country support and egg-on these immigrants. The extremist, radical, left wing SPs have done more to destroy this country from within than has any other outside group. In my opinion, these "politically correct" people are traitors of our great country.

> **With citizenship comes responsibility.**

Become a Proud American. I am an American of Japanese Ancestry (AJA). However, I do not support Japan over the United States on anything ... nada, zip, zilch, nothing, zero. *I am an American and am very proud of it.* I was born and raised in the State of Hawaii. I support America over Japan or any other country for that matter. The only things Japanese about me are my middle and last names and my love for Japanese food. However, I do not speak, understand, write, or read the Japanese language. American English is my language.

> **I am an American and am very proud of it.**

Love and Serve This Country. *I love our American Flag.* I pledge allegiance to it and to our republic for which it stands, which is a nation under God. I served on active duty in the United States Air Force for over eight years and am very proud of my service to my country. I exited the Air Force with the rank of captain. I am a Christian, not a Buddhist, Taoist, or member of any other Far Eastern religion. I am married to a wonderful Caucasian woman from Ohio, and we have three wonderful children and four grandchildren.

> **I love our American flag.**

Don't Tear Down Our Country. *I get very irritated with those who tear down the United States and who will not support our country ... especially in wartime.* I consider these folks as traitors. They do not deserve to be called American citizens. They are as bad as our enemies ... if not worse. At least when someone is our enemy, we know what to expect from him/her. These insidious, wretched people, who call themselves loyal American patriots, yet they work actively to destroy us from within. They represent a real cancer to the body that needs to be weeded out and deported to where they believe exists a better society. I'm sorry, but that's the way I feel about these losers who try everything in their power to undermine, tear down, and destroy this great country of ours.

Yes, they should either become loyal Americans or leave for those countries they feel to be better. That's the only way they will ever realize what a great thing they had left behind.

I Want My Country Back!

Rick Roberts, ace 760 KFMB AM talk show host, said, "*The southern border, more than any other border, needs to be secured tomorrow. For all those that wish to come to this country to take advantage of*

> *I get very irritated with those who tear down the United States and who will not support our country ... especially in wartime.*

her opportunity, to live under a constitution—a living document that breathes in and out just [as] you do—this country is not for sale. I should know. I'm one of the owners. You can't sell it without my permission. I want my country back!"[77]

Close and Guard Our Borders

Seal our borders. Build an electrified fence (with ribbon wire at the top) that runs clear across our northern and southern borders of the United States. Put armed military forces on our borders to keep out illegal entry of Isfasts into the United States. Give our military personnel orders to shoot anyone who fires at them first or who resists arrest. *We must secure our borders!*

> *We must secure our borders!*

---

77.   Rick Roberts, "I Want My Country Back!," extracted on 9/16/06 from URL www.mitsubishi-forums.com/t13679-i-want-my-country-back-33.htm.

Chapter 13

Politicians are Screwing Up America

Politicians never seem to put the country first. They always seek power and money before looking after the best interest of the country and its citizens. We have no statesmen anymore. We just have a bunch of political hacks who are screwing up America. Our country is in a very sad situation.

A Wake-up Letter to the RNC Chairman

Disillusioned Republican. First, I want to tell you that I have been a Republican and have voted only for Republicans over the past 40 years. However, things are changing. Yes, the Democrats are screwed up, but the Republicans are screwed up too. You guys do not know how to fight a war to win. You guys say you are for National Defense; however, you do not make a good enough effort to protect our borders. I am so disgusted with you jokers that I will not donate a penny to the Republican Party.

Listen to Your Base. You should start listening to the grass roots Republicans … your base. You will lose the support of your base in the next election if you carry on as you are doing. You are not fighting a war in the Middle East. You are just creating another Vietnam by fighting a "war of attrition." You should level cities that harbor a bulk of the al-Qaida devils. Level the cities! Sun Tzu said,

> *End the wars in Afghanistan and Iraq now by fighting to win!*

"*When you engage in actual fighting, if victory is long in coming, then men's weapons will grow dull and their ardor will be damped. If you lay siege to a town, you will exhaust your strength. Again, if the campaign is protracted, the resources of the State will not be equal to the strain. There is no instance of a country having benefited from prolonged warfare.*"[78] End the wars in Afghanistan and Iraq now by fighting to win!

Fight Wars to Win. You don't know how to fight a war to win. You should learn from the Israelis in the beginning of their war with Hezbollah. Well, it was working beautifully until the stupid Israeli politicians started to micromanage the war. If they had left it to the generals, they would have won that war instead of being embarrassed before the world audience. So, I say, turn the War in Iraq over to the generals and do not run it as a political war. If you will not do that, then bring our war fighters home, now! Sun Tzu said, "*In war, then, let your great object be victory, not lengthy campaigns.*"[79] Five years is too long to fight any war. Fight wars to win. Do not fight to endure wars-without-end.

Protect the Southern Border. *Do not call the great, patriotic American citizens who are protecting our southern borders vigilantes.* They are true Americans and true patriots. Do not send the National Guard down to the southern border only as observers. They all should be carrying weapons and ordered to use them when they are fired upon by the illegal aliens and/or drug traffickers.

> *Do not call the great, patriotic American citizens who are protecting our southern borders vigilantes.*

Need to Define the War. You cannot fight a "War on Drugs." Drugs do not fight back. It should have been a War on Drug Lords or a War on Pushers or a War on Drug Cartels. Likewise, you cannot fight a "War on Terrorism." It should be a War on Terrorists or a War on Terrorist-supporting Countries. We should fight Iran and Syria, not Iraq.

Be Proactive, Not Reactive. We should be in there helping Israel fight Hezbollah. What are you going to do … wait until they drop a nuke weapon on Haifa before we get into the fight? War with Iran, Syria, and North Korea is inevitable. Are you going to wait until they start bombing our cities in the United States before you deal with the Axis of Evil?

Democrats Will Bring War to Our Shores. Now that the Democrats have won control of Congress, they are on their way to win the presidency in the

---

78.   Sun Tzu, *The Art of War*. Extracted on 10/15/06 from The Internet Classics Archive of the Massachusetts Institute of Technology at URL: http://classics.mit.edu/Tzu/artwar.html.

79.   Ibid.

subsequent election. That result will surely bring warfare on our CONUS motherland. *We will be ushering in the Third World War under "weak-on-defense" Democrat leadership.*

Lead, Not Follow. If you truly have the strong, right leadership, then you should lead. You guys are just waiting for the next big attack to happen in our large cities before you get off your duffs and do something positive about it. Why don't you get proactive instead just asking us for more money? Money won't solve a thing because we will still have all the loser Democrats and you loser Republicans running the country. I am so disgusted with all of you that I may register as an Independent from the next election forward.

> ## We will be ushering in the Third World War under "weak-on-defense" Democrat leadership.

No Great Military Leaders or Statesmen Anymore. We do not have any great leaders anymore. We do not have any great statesmen anymore. If General George S. Patton, Jr., were here today and given the task of winning the war, we would not be in the situation in which we find ourselves. Patton would assure that we had no Isfast terrorists left. Why does the Administration not hotly pursue Osama bin Laden? Why do you not commit two divisions with the sole mission of going after that rat and bagging him within six months? Why do you let him live? That should be a top priority!

We Need Leaders! I once heard a story about a brave Army officer in the Korean War. Over 100,000 Red Chinese soldiers were attacking his battalion of less than a thousand infantrymen. This brave Army officer called back to headquarters and said, "We have them on our right; we have them on our left; we have them in front of us; and we have them behind us. We have them exactly where we want them. We are proceeding with the battle!" We need military and political leaders like this Army officer to fight our wars today. However, we do not have any. Our top military leaders have all become politicians. Our military and civilian politicians only seem to find fault with everything and everyone but themselves. They never lead. We need leaders!

Learn from the Past. Now, you will probably accuse me of being too hawkish. Mark my words! If you do not learn from the past, you will surely repeat the same mistakes in the future. George Santayana said, "*Those who cannot remember* *the past are condemned to repeat it.*"[80] We need leaders who will be like Teddy Roosevelt, who said, "*Speak softly and carry a big stick. You will go far.*" We need leaders like Ronald Reagan who tore down the Iron Curtain, destroyed the Soviet Union, and said, "*Trust but inspect.*"

Do Something! *Therefore, when are YOU going to be a leader and lead out instead of playing your silly politics as do the idiotic Democrats.* You are in charge of the country right now. So what are you doing? Apparently, you are doing nothing of significance. The Democrats get all over you people for not doing anything. You politicians (both Republican and Democrats) make me sick. The only time you will ever do anything is when our enemies directly attack us. By then, it is too little too late. Get proactive!

> *Therefore, when are YOU going to be a leader and lead out instead of playing your silly politics as do the idiotic Democrats.*

Let Generals Fight the Wars; Politicians Stay Out. Leave the fighting of wars up to our generals. All you politicians need to stay out of their hair or bring all of our boys and women in uniform back home. You do not know how to fight a war. You do not know how to protect our borders from infiltrating Al-Qaida sleeper cells. When the big nuclear bang occurs, take this letter out and read it again.

No Statesmanship. We need great leaders and statesmen in this country. Right now, I see good statesmanship displayed in neither the Democrat nor the Republican parties. Therefore, stop sending me silly emails soliciting my hard-earned money. All you guys want to do with the money is to self-perpetuate yourselves.

Term Limit. *We should have term limits with a political career limited to only one term.* That way, holding an elective office would be community service instead of careers. No politician can build a career out of politics if they must serve

> *We should have term limits with a political career limited to only one term.*

---

80.   George Santayana (16 December 1863 in Madrid, Spain—26 September 1952 in Rome, Italy), was a philosopher, essayist, poet, and novelist. Taken from *Reason in Common Sense*, the first volume of his *The Life of Reason*.

only one term. You all then would need to find a real job somewhere. Additionally, you all would not have the filthy power over which you constantly squabble. All you politicians make me so sick that I can barf. So, please stay out of my life.

Get Rid of All Politicians. I will fight our enemies when they are blowing up my neighbors' homes and beheading their children, women, and old folks with carpenter saws. By then, it will be too late for all of you sorry politicians to do anything. You all disgust me … every last one of you. The problem with our whole society is politicians. We should be rid of all of you. *We need community servants, not career politicians!*

> *We need community servants, not career politicians!*

Ripe for a Third Party. At no time in American history has our country been more ready for a third political party then right now, and I don't mean the Libertarian Party. They are such a joke making rights without responsibility as the most important thing. I mean an American Conservative Party. The Republicans have drifted too far left. We need a consistently conservative party in the United States. If one started now, I would join it.

Disgustedly,

Robert T. (Bob) Uda

Post Note: The RNC Chairman, Ken Mehlman, lost it all for the Republicans on the mid-term elections because he ignored the Republican conservative base. He resigned in shame shortly after the disgraceful loss of control of both houses of Congress. He never once answered any emails I wrote to him. I say good riddance to a weak RNC chairman.

> *We need a consistently conservative party in the United States.*

I May Be Wrong … But Not Very Much

I discuss here the differences between conservatism and liberalism as interpreted by a commoner. It also counters some of the falsehoods, diatribes, and barbs against California Governor Arnold Schwarzenegger and President George W. Bush.

Liberalism is Synonyms to Hypocrisy. Isn't it funny that when Clinton did his bad-boy deeds, the Democrats gave him a pass because of the good economy (supposedly), and he was an okay guy because it was just "all about sex (with a couple of minor exceptions, i.e., Clinton was married at the time as well as the sitting president of the United States)"? Now, a Republican (Schwarzenegger) had an similar sexual and economic background (with the exception that Arnold may have committed fornication but did not commit adultery, obstruct justice, tamper with witnesses, and lie to a grand jury as did the then sitting president of the United States, i.e., Clinton) and, according to the Democrats, Arnold's a no-good guy. *Liberalism and hypocrisy, apparently, are synonymous.*

Double Standard among Liberal Democrats. Arnold Schwarzenegger has liberal leanings. He is married to a dyed-in-the-wool Democrat. Additionally, he is a foreign-born, naturalized citizen. It seems that he should fit perfectly with the Democrats' mantra. After all, Democrats are liberal, love those of their own ilk, and want to give aliens (legal, illegal, enemies, or otherwise) driver's licenses, free social services, and the vote. However, the Democrats hate Schwarzenegger so much that they did anything and everything in their power to beat him in his two elections for the California governorship. *Apparently, there is a double standard among liberal Democrats.* However, Arnold beat them handily in both elections. Surprisingly, he accomplished that feat in the most liberal, Democrat state in the union next to Massachusetts, which also had a Republican governor (Mitt Romney). That says something about the people not wanting to have one party totally control these most left wing, ultra-liberal states.

> *Liberalism and hypocrisy, apparently, are synonymous.*

> *Apparently, there is a double standard among liberal Democrats.*

Wesley Clark. It is funny how a Republican-leaning ex-general, Wesley Clark, who voted for Republicans Ronald Reagan and Richard Nixon, and who appeared at a Republican fundraiser, is warmly accepted by Democrats and liberals as verified when he "quickly shot to the top of several national polls" during the early part of the 2004 campaign. He accomplished this feat simply by registering as a Democrat after Presidential Advisor Carl Rove did not return his call when Clark wanted to be involved with the Republicans. Apparently, liberals appear to be wishy-washy in their politics.

Arianna Huffington. Isn't it funny how ultra-liberal Arianna Huffington, former wife of an ex-Republican gubernatorial candidate of California, who recently withdrew from the race, masqueraded for years as a Republican, ran to replace fallen Governor Gray Davis, and then supported Davis to remain as Governor of California? As I said before, *liberals are wishy-washy in their politics.*

Arnold Schwarzenegger's Accusers. Isn't it funny how seven (or so) women who had claimed that they were sexually fondled by Arnold Schwarzenegger over 20 to 35 years before his first gubernatorial race never bothered to file their complaints (when the alleged infractions supposedly occurred) until less than a week before the California recall of Governor Davis vote? Isn't it funny that they are all Democrats? Isn't it strange that Arnold likes to fondle only liberals? Isn't it strange that the Democrats are comparably equating fondling to rape, adultery, fornication, and Nazism? What's wrong with that picture anyway?

> *Liberals are wishy-washy in their politics.*

Liberals Stop at Nothing. You guessed it! Apparently, liberals will lie, cheat, steal, slander, use innuendo, smear, character assassinate, burn the U.S. flag, desecrate the Oval Office, give secrets to Red China, accept political contributions from the enemy, protect the criminal over the victim, support the enemy (Saddam Hussein and Osama bin Laden), and maim to advance their cause.

Conclusion about Liberals. The only conclusion that a humble grass-roots citizen and common voter comes to by these examples above is this:

- **Raw Power.** Apparently, all liberal activists and politicians care about is raw power; they will do anything to gain, retain, and maintain it.

- **Selfishness.** Apparently, they do not really care about the commoner, the welfare of the people, or the nation. All they care about is themselves and padding their own pocket books.

- **No Moral Compass.** *Liberals will bend in any direction the wind blows.* They will follow any wind of doctrine (whatever is politically correct) as long as it advances their position. Hence, neither charges of hypocrisy nor following solid principles hinders them in any way. They have no moral compass.

- **Masses are Asses.** Apparently, all liberal politicians and activists use the masses (the econ teacher, Mr. Gross, at Kailua High School called it "the masses are asses") for their votes. They will keep them figuratively enslaved by throwing them social programs and entitlement programs to retain them as figurative indentured servants on the figurative plantation. People are fools to be

> *Liberals will bend in any direction the wind blows.*

used this way; hence, "the masses are asses." Mr. Gross was right!

Democrat to Republican. These are my personal thoughts and opinions. I may be wrong … but not very much. I started out as a registered Kennedy Democrat, became educated and wised up over time, and automatically migrated to conservatism. You cannot hold that against me!

Migration from Liberalism to Conservatism. I have resided on both sides of the fence. When I was a Democrat, I was in "a party that really cared about the common man." Now, all they care about is power, money, and themselves (just look at the Hollywood elite). I still care about the common-man, which falls more in line with conservatism today. When the Blacks, Hispanics, Native Americans, and Asians finally realize this also, they will free themselves from the psychological plantations, rich-poor Latin American dichotomy, Indian reservations, and mental WW II detention camps in the US and will migrate in droves to conservatism.

Senator Harry Reid—A Liberal's Liberal

Taking God Out of Our Pledge to the Flag. You may not be a Jay Leno fan, but I think this quote pretty much hits the nail on the head. The quote of the month by Jay Leno is as follows: "*With hurricanes, tornadoes, fires out of control, mud slides, flooding, severe thunderstorms tearing up the country from one end to another, and with the threat of bird flu and terrorist attacks, are we sure this is a good time to take God out of the Pledge of Allegiance?*"

God's Way of Expressing His Displeasure. I believe that it is God's way of telling the liberals and Democrats to get lost, cease and desist, and enough already! That man, Harry Reid, makes me very ill. I just cannot believe he is a fellow Mormon. I think he puts his politics before his Country and religious beliefs. However, he has his free agency. I don't think he will last long in politics.

Chooses Not to Be a Great Statesman. The Lord has given Harry Reid a wonderful opportunity to become a great statesman. However, he chooses to be just another typical political hack. That is unfortunate. He did not learn anything from former Mormon statesmen such as US Senator Reed Smoot, Secretary of Agriculture Ezra Taft Benson, Secretary of Housing and Urban Development (HUD) George Romney, Secretary of the Treasury David M. Kennedy, Utah Governor and Secretary of Human and Health Services (H&HS) Mike Leavitt, Massachusetts Governor Mitt Romney, et al.

> *The Lord has given Harry Reid a wonderful opportunity to become a great statesman. However, he chooses to be just another political hack.*

Extremist Liberal Democrats. Harry Reid will go down in history with cohorts of the likes of Jimmy Carter, Bill Clinton, Hillary Clinton, Ted Kennedy, Al Gore, John Kerry, Howard Dean, Barbara Boxer, Charles Schumer, Charlie Rangel, and all of the other radical, left wing, extremist, liberal Democrats. He killed the Patriot Act and bragged about it. He is for stem-cell research, which is against his religious beliefs. He is against English as the national language in the US calling it racist.

A Work of Liberal Art! He is against the Federal Marriage Amendment, which, again, is against his religious beliefs. He is for illegal aliens entering our country and taking advantage of our medical, schooling, welfare, employment, and social services. He has taken contributions from the crook Jack Abramoff. He has had shady real estate investment deals in Nevada and has received windfall profits from them. *He called President George W. Bush a "loser" before young schoolchildren*

> *He called President George W. Bush a "loser" before young schoolchildren but later recanted and apologized after catching the blast from many others.*

but later recanted and apologized after catching the blast from many others. The list of embarrassments continues on-and-on. The man is a work of liberal art!

Could Be the Breath of Fresh Air. He could be the "breath of fresh air" in the currently stench of a Democrat Party, but he chooses not to be a statesman, which is very sad. Now he is the majority leader in the US Senate. Negative things will continue to happen surrounding this man and his political party.

A Letter to Former Senator Zell Miller

The Honorable Zell Miller
United States Senator
United States Senate

September 2, 2004

Dear Senator Zell Miller,

This is a member of grassroots America writing you.

I heard/watched your speech last night on television at the Republican National Convention, and you brought tears to my eyes. You gave absolutely the best speech that I have heard in both the Democrat and Republican National Conventions. I consider you a great American and THE best Statesman in the country.

You represent the best Democrat I have ever seen/known including all of the past U.S. presidents. You are also better than 99 percent of all Republicans. If you should ever run for president in either party, this Republican conservative would certainly vote and campaign for you.

No other Democrat can earn similar support from me; however, I did vote for John Kennedy. I was a registered Democrat at that time but changed to Republican after seeing the Democrat party become more-and-more crazy, as it is today.

Because of your accurate, honest, and heartfelt speech, the liberal Democrats are now attacking you. Stay the course. We grassroots citizens are solidly behind you. Although I am 62 years old [when this letter was written back in 2004], I hope I will be as alive and as active 10 years from now as you are today.

I like you because you put your country before your party. If the Republican Party starts going too far left (as it is now heading in that direction), I will do as you do, which is to support the man who will defend our country and safety of our people before marching lock-step in line with the party. Like you, I am an American first before I am a party man (Republican in my case).

Keep up the great work you are doing. You are a breath of fresh air. We little people love you and wish you the best.

Sincerely yours,

Bob Uda

Chapter 14

Conclusions and Recommendations

This is the most important chapter of this book where the important conclusions are consolidated in one place followed by a few recommendations to the US Administration, the Congress, and the military departments.

Conclusions

Summarizing the salient points of this book, the following conclusions are made in the major areas of (1) on war, (2) threat, and (3) domestic problems.

On War

1. **On Going to War.** We should only go to war as the last resort after we explore and exercise all possible avenues. When we do go to war, Congress should officially declare war on the enemy so we know which politicians are for and which are against going to war.

2. **Go to War to Win.** When we do go to war, we should go to war to win using all means possible. No strategy or tactic will be avoided or eliminated because of political correctness. Leave winning the war to the generals. Politicians should stay out of micromanaging the generals in fighting the war.

3. **Tactical Nukes.** Tactical nuclear weapons (TNWs) should be used in ending the War on Terrorism. Many more lives will be saved by using TNWs. If we have the weapons at our disposal, we should use them. When we fight a war, we fight a war to win. We should not allow the enemy to regroup and fight another day. All-out wars should be short ... no more than 12 months long! We accomplish this end result by not hesitating to use all resources, weapons, strategies, and tactics at our disposal. Blitzkrieg war with nukes is the best way to go to end the war quickly. It saves time, money, and unnecessary loss of lives.

4. **21st Century Wars.** All 21st Century wars will be asymmetrical, asynchronous, or unconventional wars or low-intensity conflicts (LICs). Symmetrical,

synchronous, or conventional wars are 20th Century wars, which are wars of the past.

5. **War on Terrorism.** The War on Terrorism can be won through implementing the "10-Point Plan" shown in chapter 4 of this book. This plan includes the following:

    - Officially Declare War
    - Generals to Fight the War
    - One Goal: To Win at All Cost
    - Keep Politicians Out
    - Discard Geneva Convention
    - Bring Traitors to Trial
    - Level Terrorist Rat Holes with Tactical Nukes
    - Use Enemy Uniform
    - Apply Martial Law
    - Fight Fire with Fire

    The problem we would have with implementing this Plan is that the secular progressives (SPs); extremist, left wing, radical liberals; and Democrats would fight tooth-and-nail the eight points represented by bullets number 1, 2, 3, 4, 5, 6, 7, and 8. The only time they will ever relent and change their minds is when it is obvious that we will be overrun and conquered. By then, it will be too late. That is our national dilemma.

6. **World War III.** We are currently in a worldwide war with Islamo-fascists (Isfasts). The Isfasts have fought battles in the United States, United Kingdom, France, Germany, Spain, The Philippines, Russia, China, Chechnya, Israel, Kuwait, Lebanon, Saudi Arabia, Afghanistan, Iraq, India, Pakistan, Indonesia, Somalia, Venezuela, and many other countries of the world. In addition the countries listed above, Isfast cells currently operate in Canada, Mexico, Australia, Japan, Italy, Egypt, United Arab Emirates, Sicily, Syria, Ethiopia, and many, many other countries of the world. Indeed, we are in a world war. When the Isfasts explode nuclear bombs in our major cities, World War III will go into full swing. We must then go after the Isfasts' juggler vein, or we will be at risk of being conquered, placed in bondage, or annihilated.

7. **United Nations.** The UN is a useless, worthless organization that is detrimental to the well-being of the United States. The UN is run by a bunch of cheats, liars, and thieves. UN workers from many anti-American countries of the world break our laws, commit espionage on us, and undermine our position on the world scene.

8. **Neo Axis of Evil.** Under the current leadership of those countries, war with Iran, Syria, and North Korea is inevitable. These leaders must be removed and replaced with more stable, rational, and respectable leaders.

9. **Al-Jazeera and CNN.** Al-Jazeera and the Communist (or Cable) News Network (CNN) represent the right arm and left arm of al-Qaida, Taliban, Hamas, Hezbolla, and all other Isfasts.

10. **Lessons Unlearned.** We have not learned any lessons from the Vietnam War. Refer to Robert McNamara's 11 Lessons from Vietnam in chapter 2 of this book. We violate every one of those lessons as we fight our current asymmetrical wars in Afghanistan, Iraq, and the War on Terrorism.

11. **Generals.** We have no "real" generals today who knows how to win wars. Where is General George S. Patton, Jr., when we need him?

12. **Leading the War.** If politicians and generals want to go to war, they should don the uniform and personally lead the troops into battle. That is what true leaders of old did. Why should we not continue that brave practice?

Threat

13. **Isfast Threat.** Isfasts present a real threat to the United States and the world. Hence, they must be eradicated.

14. **Isfast Goals.** The Isfasts consist of members of al-Qaida, Taliban, Hamas, Hezbolla, and extremist, radical, fundamentalist Muslims who are the followers of the Islamic faith. The Isfasts are out to dominate the world, convert everyone to Islam, and kill all infidels and non-believers, which include all Americans, Europeans, Westerners, Christians, Jews, and hypocrites (i.e., those Arabs-Muslims-Islamites (AMIs) who do not tow the party line).

15. **Isfast Destiny.** The only language Isfasts understand is to kill or be killed. They believe that if they are killed, they will receive 72 virgins in the afterlife. We must grant them their wish. We should have a "take no prisoners" policy. Why waste the time, effort, and money on lengthy, costly trials? We should

not capture any terrorists but instead kill all of them on sight. Capturing Saddam Hussein was a mistake. We should have killed him in his spider hole. However, fortunately, we did it right with killing "the butcher" Abu Musab al-Zarqawi.

16. **AMIs.** The Isfasts have hijacked the Islamic religion. About 10 to 15 percent of all AMIs side with the Isfasts. That ranges anywhere from 100 million to 150 million AMIs! That presents a formidable problem for the West.

17. **Pigmy Not Giant Anymore.** If Japan attacked the United States today, they would probably win. Why is that? Because the SPs and extremist, left wing, radical liberals have made our country weak, Godless, and divided in the eyes of the world. We are no more a sleeping giant. We are now a sleeping pigmy.

Domestic Problems

18. **The Enemy Within.** The enemy within (including disloyal AMIs; SPs; and extremist, left wing, radical liberals) are ruining our country. Something must be done about them.

19. **Traitorous Behavior.** We have too many people in Congress, the press, Hollywood, and the education system that display traitorous behavior. If we were in a truly declared war, say World War III, we would arrest, jail, try, convict, and execute these traitors for aiding and abetting the enemy and conducting acts detrimental to the safety, security, and well-being of the United States of America. Where is Joseph McCarthy when we need him? We need him to clean out the Hollywood Mafia, liberal universities, errant media (CNN and *New York Times*), American Communist-Leaning (or Civil Liberties) Union (ACLU), Amnesty International (AI), and Council on American-Islamic Relations (CAIR).

20. **Politics and Politicians.** Politics and politicians have reduced themselves to the lowest level I have ever seen in my entire life (64 years). Most politicians are crooks, liars, and cheats. Politicians are less respected than used-car salesmen, fallen evangelical religious leaders, and pedophile priests. Politicians are screwing up America!

21. **Congress.** Congress needs a major overhaul. We should have only one term for both US senators and US representatives. Nobody should be able to make a career out of politics. US senators and congressmen should be one-term "community service" positions. That's it! After they serve their one

term, they then need to go find a "real job." That will eliminate all of the shenanigans that currently go on in politics. There should be an "up-or-out" policy. In other words, they can only run for the next higher office or go find a real job.

22. **Democrats.** The extremist, radical, liberal Democrats are "weak on defense" with their "cut-and-run strategy." Generally, they are anti-American, anti-military, and anti-war pacifists. Jack Murtha is the worst of the worst followed by John Kerry, Ted Kennedy, Howard Dean, Nancy Pelosi, Al Gore, Al Sharpton, Chuck Schumer, Charlie Rangel, and Harry Reid.

23. **SPs and Radical Liberals.** The SPs and extremist, left wing, radical liberals secretively want the US to lose the wars in Afghanistan and Iraq. They work feverishly to make us lose the War on Terrorism by their anti-American and "blame-America-first" rhetoric. All they do is to re-energize and motivate the Isfasts to continue their fight.

24. **Disloyal Opposition.** There is no loyal opposition any more. There is only a disloyal opposition. The extremist, left wing, radical liberals have done this to our legislative branch of government. The only time we saw any semblance of unity was in the week following 9/11. After that, it was business as usual. Sad.

25. **No Unity.** The president and commander-in-chief cannot succeed in fighting and winning a war if the disloyal opposition continuously fights him tooth-and-nail on everything he tries to do to wage a successful war. President Lincoln said, *"A house divided against itself cannot stand."* They don't listen to President Abraham Lincoln. If both political parties work together, they can accomplish anything. If they do not work together, they will accomplish nothing of significance. We are in a very sad state of affairs. This is why we cannot and will not win the War on Terrorism under the current leadership of both political parties.

26. **Courts.** The legal system is messed up and totally dysfunctional. Liberal judges legislate from the bench. They are soft on criminals and show little or no concern for victims. The court system leaves a lot to be desired.

27. **Entitlement Programs.** Entitlement programs are a crock. They only keep the downtrodden further downtrodden. Entitlements comprise a strategy that the extremist, left wing, radical liberals use to keep the lower class on the figurative plantation.

28. **Political Correctness.** Political correctness has been detrimental to America. If you fight a politically correct war, you might just as well surrender. There is no way you can win.

29. **Collateral Damage.** In war, there should be no such thing as concern for collateral damage. We were never concerned about it during World War II when we dropped two atomic bombs on Hiroshima and Nagasaki. We were not concerned about it when we bombed Dresden and other Germany cities. Why are we concerned about collateral damage now in asymmetrical warfare? We just play into the hands of the enemy.

30. **Racial Profiling.** With the exception of the Oklahoma City domestic terrorist bombing by Timothy McVeigh, nearly every other Isfast terrorist incident that has occurred throughout the world has been committed by Isfast AMIs between the ages of 17 and 40. Hence, we should apply racial profiling to identify and capture Isfasts in the United States before they can commit their dastardly deeds. The FBI should identify, gather data on, prepare dossiers on, track, and monitor all known Isfasts in the United States.

31. **Geneva Convention.** The Geneva Convention is obsolete; hence, we should discard it. The Isfasts do not subscribe to or adhere to the Geneva Convention. Therefore, they should not be protected by the Geneva Convention. Not a single animal in the Animal Kingdom is protected under the Geneva Convention. So, why should Isfast animals be protected under the Geneva Convention? These are the lowest of low life of the world. They deserve to receive the same kind of treatment and justice that they dish out to all of the unfortunate people they torture, behead, burn, butcher, and mutilate. Fair is fair.

32. **Borders.** The border situation is a real disaster. Illegal aliens, including Isfasts, are entering the United States in droves through our porous, unguarded borders.

33. **Illegal Aliens.** This is a major problem in this country. There appears to be very little to no political will by our elected politicians to solve this problem just because both political parties seek the illegal alien vote. Indeed, that is a very sad situation.

34. **Errant Press.** We need freedom "from" the press, not freedom "of" the press. The errant press has gone beyond the pale. They are political organizations

that advance the liberal agenda. They do not present real news … just political diatribe, spin, and SP ideology. That's why I don't watch the mainstream, rather lame-stream, media any more, and I never read those big-city liberal newspapers. I get my news from talk radio and the Internet. Additionally, I don't go to the movies anymore because of the garbage that the Hollywood elite produces. Why should I pay to watch trash?

35. **Pacifists.** Pacifists aid and abet the enemy and are, therefore, traitors to our country.

36. **Statesmen.** We have no real statesmen in politics today … people like Ronald Reagan, Gerald Ford, Dwight D. Eisenhower, Franklin D. Roosevelt, and Theodore Roosevelt. Statesmen place the country and the people before their political party and petty politics. Unfortunately, we have nothing but political hacks in government, i.e., politicians who participate in aimless political activity.

37. **Mitt Romney.** Mitt Romney could win the presidency in 2008 if he played his cards right. Appendix E of this book provides suggestions on how to make it happen. Mitt Romney could probably be our next statesman president.

Recommendations

These few recommendations are made for consideration by the US Government if our leaders are interested in winning the War on Terrorism.

Recommendation #1: United Front—Get the two major political parties to work together, to cooperate, and to be united in the war effort. Lack of cooperation and teamwork have contributed to our failings in the wars in Afghanistan and Iraq as well as the overall War on Terrorism.

Recommendation #2: Declaration of War—Get Congress to declare war officially on the Islamo-fascists (Isfasts). This officially identifies those in Congress who are for and who are against winning the war. Call the war the "War on Isfasts."

Recommendation #3: Generals—Let the Joint Chiefs of Staff (JCS), led by its Chairman (CJCS), run the war effort. Give them the mandate to win the war at all cost and within 12 months. If they cannot do it in 12 months, replace them with generals who can accomplish the mission. After 6 months, it will become clear whether the JCS will be able to accomplish the mission or not. Any and all weapons (including nukes), strategies, and tactics are available for their use and are allowable. Provide them with the necessary and sufficient resources that they need to accomplish the mission. Politicians shall stay out of micromanaging the war effort. Do not take any prisoners. Kill all Isfasts on sight. Do not fight a "politically correct" war. War is hell. Therefore, anything and everything goes. Fight fire with fire.

Recommendation #4: Frivolous Wars—If we enter frivolous wars, the politicians' children/grandchildren must be recruited first to fight those silly wars. In addition, those politicians who voted to go to war shall be required to wear military uniforms and lead the battles in those silly wars.

Recommendation #5: Overhaul the Three Branches of Government—Overhaul Congress. Establish term limits to one term. Make serving in Congress as "community service," not a political career. Apply the "up-or-out" technique. Overhaul the courts and the legal system. Provide the line-item veto to the US president.

Recommendation #6: The Enemy Within—Ferret out "the enemy within." Bring suspected traitors to trial and execute those who are found guilty.

Recommendation #7: United Nations—Withdraw the United States from the United Nations (UN). Physically kick the UN out of New York and the US. Form a coalition of friendly Western nations starting with the United States, Great Britain, Israel, Canada, Australia, Japan, Taiwan, South Korea, The Philippines, India, Pakistan, Italy, Germany, Spain, France, Saudi Arabia, UAE, Kuwait, and other such friendly nations. Call it the United Free Nations (UFN). Keep a jaundiced eye on a few of those in the above list. Stop giving money and weapons to unfriendly and untrustworthy nations.

Recommendation #8: Regime Change—Create regime changes in Syria, Iran, and North Korea. Target the leaders of these countries. We did it in Iraq. We can do it again in these three totalitarian countries.

Recommendation #9: Geneva Convention—Discard the Geneva Convention unless the enemy abides by its tenets. The Isfasts will never abide by its tenets. Therefore, the Geneva Convention does not apply to Isfasts. Eradicate them at will. If they torture our war-fighters, we torture their war-fighters. If they play dirty, we play dirty. All is fair in love and war.

Recommendation #10: Racial Profiling—Allow racial profiling for the duration of the "War on Isfasts." Identify and track all suspected Isfasts within the US.

Recommendation #11: Collateral Damage—Eliminate the use of the term "collateral damage." In all-out war, there is no such thing as collateral damage. Bomb whatever is required to destroy the enemy's capability and will to sustain conflict.

Recommendation #12: Illegal Aliens and Border Control—Stop illegal aliens from entering our borders. Eliminate illegal immigration. Build a high, electrified fence. Place armed guards on the borders with orders to shoot to kill if fired upon first by drug traffickers and illegal alien traffickers.

Recommendation #13: Immigration—Make English the official language of the USA. All legal immigrants shall learn the English language. All immigrants shall assimilate into American society.

Final Words

Implementing these 13 recommendations requires strong leadership, audacity (General George Patton kind), and intestinal fortitude. If our Administration and elected political leaders do not possess the political will to make these things happen, then we will have a government that is "business as usual." The War will continue on as it does. Our financial resources will become depleted. Political infighting will continue on indefinitely. The enemy will gain the upper hand on us.

Only when it becomes obvious that the United States will be conquered by the Isfasts, that's when our elected officials will attempt to do these recommendations. Then it will be too little too late. We citizens will be left to our own to fight the enemy. The Constitution of the United States of American will hang by a thread. The only way we will be saved is if, by then, we have not totally eliminated God from our Country. If we did, AMEN.

Appendix A

Patton's Speech to the Third Army

Here is a version of the speech that General George S. Patton, Jr., gave to the Third Army in England on May 31, 1944.

"Now I want you to remember that no bastard ever won a war by dying for his country. You won it by making the other poor dumb bastard die for his country. Men, all this stuff you've heard about America not wanting to fight, wanting to stay out of the war, is a lot of horse dung. Americans traditionally love to fight. ALL REAL Americans, love the sting of battle. When you were kids, you all admired the champion marble shooter, the fastest runner, the big league ball players, the toughest boxers.

"Americans love a winner and will not tolerate a loser. Americans play to win all the time. I wouldn't give a hoot in Hell for a man who lost and laughed. That's why Americans have never lost and will never lose a war. Because the very thought of losing is hateful to Americans.

"No, an army is a team. It lives, eats, sleeps, fights as a team. This individuality stuff is a bunch of crap. The bilious bastard who wrote that stuff about individuality for the *Saturday Evening Post* don't know anything more about real battles than they do about fornicating.

"Now we have the finest food and equipment, the best spirit, and the best men in the world. You know … My God, I actually pity those poor bastards we're going up against. My God, I do. We're not just going to shoot the bastards, we're going to cut out their living guts and use them to grease the treads of our tanks. We're going to murder those lousy Hun bastards by the bushel.

"Now some of you boys, I know, are wondering whether or not you'll chicken out under fire. Don't worry about it. I can assure you that you'll all do your duty. The Nazis are the enemy. Wade into them. Spill their blood; shoot them in the belly. When you put your hand into a bunch of goo, that a moment before was your best friend's face, you'll know what to do.

"Now, there's another thing I want you to remember. I don't want to get any messages saying that we are holding our position. We're not holding anything; we'll let the Hun do that. We are advancing constantly, and we're not interested in holding onto anything except the enemy. We're going to hold onto him by the nose, and we're going to kick him in the ass. We're going to kick the hell out of him all the time, and we're going to go through him like crap through a goose.

"Now, there's one thing that you men will be able to say when you get back home, and you may thank God for it. Thirty years from now when you're sitting around your fireside with your grandson on your knee, and he asks you, "What did you do in the great World War Two?" You won't have to say, "Well, I shoveled shit in Louisiana." All right, you sons of bitches, you know how I feel. Oh! I would be proud to lead you wonderful guys into battle anytime, anywhere. That's all."

Appendix B

Greatest Political & Military Geniuses

Here is a brief listing of some of, in my opinion, the greatest political and military strategists and tacticians of all time. I'm sure there are many others that can be included, but these geniuses impress me the most.

Years	Politician, Strategist, Tactician	Comments
500-320 BC	Sun Tzu	Name used by the unknown Chinese authors of the sophisticated treatise on philosophy, logistics, espionage, strategy, and tactics known as The Art of War. It stresses the unpredictability of battle, the importance of deception and surprise, the close relationship between politics and military policy, and the high costs of war. The futility of seeking hard and fast rules and the subtle paradoxes of success are major themes. Sun Tzu says, "The best battle is the battle that is won without being fought."
1469-1527	Niccolo Machiavelli	The Prince, a landmark discourse on political science. The patron saint of power. Italian author and statesman. One of the outstanding figures of the Renaissance. Machiavelli believed that we should fear rather than love leaders. The people will never be satisfied if their leader makes generous promises.
1584-1645	Miyamoto Musashi	A Book of Five Rings (Go Rin No Sho), a book on strategy, tactics, and philosophy. Famous, legendary Japanese swordsman. Believed to have been one the most skilled swordsmen in history.

1780-1831	Karl von Clausewitz	On War. Prussian general and military strategist. An original thinker most influenced by the Napoleonic wars in which he fought. His most famous dictum, that war "is merely the continuation of policy by other means," emphasizes his conception of war as one part of normal and pragmatic politics.
1885-1945	George S. Patton, Jr.	The greatest military genius and US Army general of World War II. Commander of the famous US Third Army. "Old Blood and Guts" Patton was primarily known as a tank general. He was also a leading expert on amphibious landings. He had the gift of leadership and inspired his men to be much better than they actually were causing them to win every battle in which they fought.
1910-1978	Bernard Brodie	The Absolute Weapon (1946), the first book on nuclear strategy. American military strategist who was a strategic theorist at the Rand Corporation (1951-66). He concentrated on the significance of airpower in the nuclear age. He advocated a policy of deterrence.
1922-1983	Herman Kahn	On Thermonuclear War (1961). American military strategist who believed that nuclear war could be won (unlike Brodie). Graduate work in physics at Cal Tech. Worked at the Rand Corporation. In 1961, he founded the Hudson Institute.
1942-present	Michael Savage	The Savage Nation (2003), The Enemy Within (2004), Liberalism is a Mental Disorder (2005), and The Political Zoo (2006)—all New York Times bestsellers. Dr. Michael Allen Weiner (pseudonym Michael Savage)—a very controversial American talk radio host. A multiple best-selling author and political commentator. Simply put, Michael Savage is a genius of geniuses. He knows more about winning military strategy then all of the politicians and military generals put together.

Appendix C

Most Influential Talk-Radio Hosts

The list of talk-radio hosts in the order shown is from NewsMax.com (extracted on 10/6/06) in order of their influence. I have added my understanding and opinions of their political ideological leanings and my assessment of their influence. You may disagree with my assessment. That's okay. We have a right to disagree. Missing from this list are Rick Roberts and Mark Levin, two conservative talk show hosts whom I like. Levin leans towards the conservative talk-show hosts that support the Bush Administration. Roberts is more in line with Michael Savage. I personally favor Savage and Roberts.

Rank/Host	Leanings	Author's Assessment
1. Rush Limbaugh	Conservative	Supports the Bush Administration no matter what. Had a prescription drug problem.
2. Bill O'Reilly	Conservative	Supports the Bush Administration.
3. Don Imus	No consistent political leanings	Supports whomever turns him on at the moment. Sarcasm and harsh language characterizes this man.
4. Michael Savage	Conservative	Great man! Supports what's right rather than the party. Most of the other conservative radio hosts (except Rick Roberts) are jealous of him and, therefore, ignores him. They cannot even use his name when referring to him. Sad. President Bush should listen to this man.
5. Sean Hannity	Conservative	Supports the administration on almost everything except the border problem.

6. Laura Ingraham	Conservative	Impressive lady who says it like it is and really makes fools of the liberals. I really like her style.
7. Glenn Beck	Libertarian Mormon	Has been called a fringe nut propagandist who says he wants to kill Michael Moore. He can't really be all that bad.
8. Dr. Laura Schlessinger	Conservative	I agree with her at least 95 percent of the time. She is honest and straightforward in her analysis of mentally and emotionally sick people.
9. Neal Boortz	Libertarian, fiscal conservative, liberal on social issues	O'Reilly called him a "vicious SOB" on *The O'Reilly Factor*. This guy is all over the place. You can't really tell what he is. He is somewhat like Don Imus.
10. Al Franken	Liberals' Liberal	This guy epitomizes Dr. Michael Savage's assertion that "Liberalism is a mental disorder." Franken is a real mental case.
11. Mike Gallagher	Conservative	Good man on radio and Fox News.
12. Mancow	Don't know	Crazy man who got booted off his talk show in San Francisco Area. More of an entertainer than political commentator.
13. Howard Stern	Liberal	Represents everything Satanic. His audience comprise the dregs of the earth.
14. Bill Bennett	Conservative	Good man. Wrote a best-selling book, which was a compendium of great sayings and motivational stories. Got into ethical controversy with his gambling addiction.
15. Opie and Anthony	Liberals	Weirdoes
16. Ed Schultz	Liberal	Whacko
17. Michael Medved	Neo-conservative	He is against the Hollywood elite culture; hence, he can't be all that bad.

18.Randi Rhodes	Liberal	Air America whacko
19.Jim Bohannon	Liberal	Strange man
20.G. Gordon Liddy	Conservative	Represents the darker side of conservatism.
21.Diane Rehm	Liberal	NOW supporter
22.Larry Elder	Libertarian-conservative	Pre-eminent black talk show host. Good man!
23.Michael Reagan	Conservative	Should be higher on this totem. Son of President Reagan. Good man!
24.Tammy Bruce	Conservative	Don't know for sure whether she is a conservative by convenience or what. An expressed lesbian.
25.Tom Leykis	Can't tell.	Whacko and marital loser.

Appendix D

Multiple Spellings of Arabic Words & Names

Here is a brief listing of some of the numerous ways Arabic words and names are spelled, which makes communicating confusing and difficult.

Generally Accepted Way	The Numerous Other Spellings of the Same Word or Name
al-Jazeera	al Jazeera, Al Jazeera, Al-jazeera, Al-Jazeera, Al-Jazeerah, Al-Jazira, Al-jezeera, al-Gazeera, Aljazeera
al-Qaida	al Qaida, Al Qaida, al-Qaeda, al Qaeda, or Al Qaeda
Faluga	Falluga, Falugah, Fallugah, Faluja, Falujah, Falluja, Fallujah
Hezbollah	Hizbullah, Hizballah
Muhammad	Muhammed, Mohammad, Mohammed, Muhamad, Muhamed, Mohamad, Mohamed, and Mahomet
Muslim	Moslem
Osama bin Laden	Usama bin Laden
Quran	Qu'ran, Quraan, Koran, Koraan, Qoraan, Qoran
Shiite	Shia, Shiah
Sunni	Suni

Appendix E

Mitt Romney May Be Best Hope for Future

There is only one presidential candidate who shows signs of being a real statesman. Only one presidential candidate, if he wins, can lead us to win the War on Terrorism and to achieve a world of peace. That person is former Massachusetts Governor Mitt Romney. However, can Mitt Romney, a devout Mormon, be elected? The answer is "yes" but only if he runs a winning campaign, i.e., taking the high road. If the country is ready for a woman president and a black president, it is also ready for a Mormon president.

Support a Person's Values and Beliefs, not His Religion. First, I do want to point out emphatically that I will not support a politician just because he is a Mormon. To wit, I would never support Harry Reid for anything including dogcatcher. As far as I am concerned, he is an embarrassment.

Listen to Your Grass-roots Base. I do not support politicians with monetary contributions because, apparently, that is all they want from their base and supporters, i.e., money. However, I will support decent politicians (which, unfortunately, are very few-and-far-between) with my time, talents, and everything else. To me, the RNC and Ken Mehlman were a real joke … they only wanted our money, but they never, ever listen to their "grass roots" Republican base, which comprised a major *faux pas* and an Achilles heel for them in the midterm elections. When the Republicans went down to defeat, this was the reason why they lost. Lesson learned: Listen to your grass-roots base, RNC!

> *If the country is ready for a woman president and a black president, it is also ready for a Mormon president.*

Deal with Issues Head On. I will support Mitt Romney to a huge extent IF he does not take the approach as that Mormon millionaire on the West Coast did in the recent election seeking the convicted bribe-taker Ex-Congressman Duke

Cunningham's vacancy after he resigned in shame. This candidate made such a strong (sarcasm applied here) impression on me such that I cannot even remember his name! The guy was naive. The reasons why he lost were because he:

- Wanted not to appear to be a Mormon
- Ran a "politically correct" campaign
- Tried to satisfy everyone and ended satisfying no one
- Never hit issues head on

Deal with the Mormon Issue Head On. Mitt Romney needs to hit the Mormon question head on. He should not apologize for being a good Mormon. He should do everything opposite to what Harry Reid does. *Mitt Romney should position himself as a statesman instead of a political hack and political prostitute.*

Don't Make the Same Mistake Your Dad Made. I remember back when his dad (George Romney who was my hero) had the election "in the bag" and was at the top of the polls until he visited Vietnam and made the unfortunate remark that he was "brainwashed." Dumb! His campaign went down the tubes from that

> *Mitt Romney should position himself as a statesman instead of a political hack and political prostitute.*

moment forward. Mitt should not make such victory-limiting remarks like that of his dad. Furthermore, he needs to guard against the Kerry "flip-flopping" Syndrome.

Take the High Road—What a Novel Idea! Know the definition of terms used in speeches! Avoid the current blood sport of running a negative campaign. It would be a "breath of fresh air" if Mitt Romney took the high road. *Mitt should run a decent campaign based on the issues and adhering to uplifting facts, ideas, and plans. What a novel idea!*

Pro-activity Required. There is no doubt in my mind that Hillary Clinton or any of the other extremist, liberal politicians who ends up being the final Democrat contender for president WILL take the low road and attack Mitt Romney on all of the Mormon issues. Hence, Mitt's campaign need to be proactive and introduce all of these issues first and hit them head on. He should define himself before his opponent defines him. To wit, he can effectively use in campaign ads those ignorant people displaying their anti-Mormon attitudes on focus-group videos. Then, he can follow that by showing them with a changed viewpoint after they learn the truth.

Centerpiece of the Campaign. For example, we can show the ignorant comment made about the Christmas tree and Easter egg hunt as events held at Mitt Romney's home with his Mormon children, grandchildren, and relatives. Show normal Christian activities as normal Mormon activities, which represent the truth. Fight ignorance, lies, untruths, innuendo, and other such secular progressive (SP) tactics with the truth. The truth will set those ignorant voters free to vote for a good Mormon.

> *Mitt should run a decent campaign based on the issues and adhering to uplifting facts, ideas, and plans. What a novel idea!*

This approach is an effective way to promulgate paradigm shifts among all of the religiously ignorant voters out there in the Bible-Belt area of the United States. Do not make the mistake of providing alcoholic beverages for non-Mormons to drink at political events. *Being a good Mormon should be a centerpiece of Mitt Romney's campaign.*

> *Being a good Mormon should be a centerpiece of Mitt Romney's campaign.*

Winning the War on Terror Requires a Fresh, New Approach. Another thing: The War on Terror started out fine with the attacks on the Taliban in Afghanistan and Saddam Hussein's Republican Guard in Iraq. However, since those victories, we have gone very wrong in attempting to fight a continuous war of attrition, i.e., attrition of our troops, not of the enemy fighters (Taliban, al-Qaida, Hezbollah, Hamas, and other such Isfasts).

This book provides a provocative strategy to win the War on Terrorism, not to continue the huge mistakes we are currently making in Afghanistan and Iraq as well as on our borders. Mitt cannot and should not take the current Administration's strategy of maintaining and holding the current approach to fighting Isfasts. *"Stay the course" is a loser's strategy.* He needs to take an entirely new, fresh

> *"Stay the course" is a loser's strategy.*

approach at fighting the War on Terror. You can extract much of that new approach from this book.

Don't Follow the Warn-out Republican Approach. The Republicans took a thumping in the mid-term elections because they would not listen to their base. I tell you this: Mitt Romney has a chance to win the presidency in 2008 if he will follow these "10 Points for Victory":

1. **Mormon Issue.** Face the Mormonism issue head on. Do not shy away from it. Get proactive. Define himself as a Christian; don't let others define him. Be proud to be a Mormon. Don't try to hide it like that Mormon who tried to win the vacancy of that defamed Ex-Congressman Duke "the Crook" Cunningham who took bribes and resigned in shame when he was caught red-handed. I could not support a man like that. He had a lot of money, but he did not have any guts.

2. **Statesman.** Be a statesman as he is currently doing. Don't transition into a combative candidate. Avoid being like Harry Reid. He is an embarrassment.

3. **Positive Campaign.** Refrain from negative campaigning. The populace is tired of it. Run a proactive, positive, constructive campaign.

4. **Iraq War.** Win the war in Iraq quickly (and I mean "win" the war) and bring our troops home. Wipe out the Sunni Triangle. Wipe out al-Sadr and his army. Destroy all channels of war materials being shipped into Iraq from Syria and Iran. Hit the sources of war-making materials.

5. **Alternative Fuel.** Establish a top-priority program similar to the "Manhattan Project" to find an alternative to gasoline for running our automobiles. Set a 10-year goal. If President John Kennedy could get us to the moon in 10 years, we certainly can find an alternative fuel in 10 years.

6. **Illegal Aliens.** End the illegal alien problem. Build the fence. Put "real" troops on the border. Arrest those illegal aliens who violate the law and throw them into prison. Arrest those who employ illegal aliens and levy very severe fines and jail terms for company executives.

7. **Conservatism.** Be a strong Ronald Reagan-type conservative (or, better yet, a Barry Goldwater-type conservative) and run a campaign to win back the conservative, Republican base, which they had lost in the recent disastrous midterm elections.

8. **War on Terrorism.** Win the overall War on Terrorism quickly. Get Osama bin Laden quickly. Round up the al-Qaida members from within the United States and incarcerate them in prison. Put the squeeze on both Iran and North Korea and disarm them of nuclear weapons or the capability to build nuclear weapons.

9. **Family Values.** Run a "real" and "true" family-values campaign. Turn back the socialism and secular progressivism that has been creeping upon us for the past half century. Put God back into our republic.

10. **Spending.** Reduce spending as he did with the Winter Olympics in Salt Lake City and as governor of Massachusetts. Reduce the size of government. No new taxes! Reduce frivolous pork barrel spending.

Put Substance Into the "Run Mitt Run" Slogan. There you go. If we can convince Mitt Romney to run his campaign following the above "10 Points for Victory," voters will elect him President of the United States of America in 2008.

If he attempts to run a "middle-of-the-road" campaign, he will lose. If he runs a "politically correct" campaign, he will lose. If he speaks with forked tongue, he will lose. If he runs a nasty, negative, destructive campaign, he will lose. If he compromises his religious beliefs, his principles, his ethics, and his values, he will lose. If he flip-flops on major issues, he will lose.

He needs to formulate a battle cry that will define himself and his candidacy and not let the Democrats define him. Then, the "Run Mitt Run" slogan will have some substance to it.

Note: On January 1, 2007, the "Run Mitt Run" slogan transitioned into becoming the "Our Shared Values" slogan.

First Major Error. The first big error that Mitt Romney can make is to hire Alex Castellanos as his image-maker. Do not do it! This guy will run a very sick, negative, destructive campaign. Some may believe that a negative campaign is more successful than a positive campaign. However, grassroots Americans are really getting sick, tired, and turned-off with the way the negative campaigns went in the most recent midterm elections.

> *Have you ever thought of the company that creates all of those very effective MormonAds?*

Castellanos will Make Mitt Lose. Castellanos lost Bob Dole's campaign for president. He caused Jeb Bush to lose the governor's race against Lawton Chiles the first time he ran against him. In the 1998 campaign for governor of Ohio, Bob Taft had to pull an ad that Castellanos riddled with untruths. These are only a few examples of this ignorant man's methods … and people think he is great. Excuse me!

Be Above the Frey. No, you do not want this knucklehead hack to create Mitt Romney's image. There are better image-makers out there. *Have you ever thought of the company that creates all of those very effective MormonAds?* This guy (Castellanos) will be a disaster for Mitt Romney. This loser of an image-maker will use blood-sport ads to create a very negative image of Mitt Romney. On the other hand, *a successful image-maker will use subtle methods, tactics, and strategies of discrediting the opponent yet building up Mitt Romney in people's eyes.* The brute force approach to campaign ads will not work in the next presidential election. Subtle ads that bring out the bald truth against Mitt's opponent while making Mitt appear to be above the fray (a true statesman) will be the successful way to go.

Castellanos is a Loser. Mark my words! If this supposed expert, Castellanos, is hired and then Mitt loses, you heard it here first. Castellanos is a loser. He will mold Mitt Romney into a loser. I believe that with all of my heart, might, mind, and soul.

> *A successful image-maker will use subtle methods, tactics, and strategies of discrediting the opponent yet building up Mitt Romney in people's eyes.*

That is my premonition. Get a better image-maker. There are good ones out there.

Run a Dirty Campaign and Lose. If Mitt Romney runs a dirty, negative campaign, he will lose. That is my promise to you. He will be no better than Harry Reid of Nevada, who (sadly) became the majority leader of the US Senate in January 2007. Mitt Romney should image himself as a statesman … direct, honest, full of integrity, calm under pressure, objective, a great American, and loving.

Disarm Your Detractors. Think of how Ronald Reagan carried himself. He always was affable, smiling, and never got confrontational like all of the Bozo politicians do these days. Whenever he got in trouble, he always made a joke of it that dissolved people's bad attitude against him. Indeed, he gave his detractors an uplifting experience that disarmed them. They laughed along with the self-deprecating jokes that Reagan made towards himself. How can anyone hate Ronald after he did that? Ronald Reagan was a true statesman. That is how Mitt Romney should pattern himself.

Think Outside of the Box. The idea of a third-party attack machine is a plausible one, but it is not the answer. "Think outside of the box" for a second. It should be a fourth party that should do the task. Approach #3 using an independent political organization is not the winning answer. You need Approach #4, which is a fourth party. That is the winning answer. *That fourth party is not an organized political organization, but, instead, it is "We the people."* We can organize individuals all across this great land to conduct a coordinated effort to do the following:

> *That fourth party is not an organized political organization, but, instead, it is "We the people."*

- Individuals to write positive letters to the editor about Mitt Romney
- Writers to write pro-Romney op-ed pieces and articles for newspapers and magazines
- Individuals to prepare positive videos on Mitt Romney
- Authors to write constructive books on Mitt Romney
- Individuals to go house to house passing out positive literature
- Individuals to hold cottage meetings, parties, media events, etc.
- Individuals to hold focus groups
- Grass-roots Americans to spread the word through the Internet and talk radio
- Individuals to take out ads in newspapers, magazines, radio spots, TV commercials, and billboards in support of Mitt Romney
- College Young Republicans to go all out on the campaign
- This list can go on and on and on

Bottom-up Campaign. The point here is that we need to get individual citizens, the grass-root Republican base, and all interested parties involved in this campaign. It needs to be a bottom-up campaign, not a top-down campaign. You would be surprised how successful individuals can be when everyone pulls in the same direction. Political hacks and party operatives should not run Romney's campaign. Instead, the grassroots conservative base should run it as "of the people, by the people, and for the people." He must take that strategy to surface as the winner.

Not "Politics as Usual." *Mitt Romney must be a uniter, not a divider.* He must not run a polarizing campaign. He must be like Ronald Reagan, where more people will be for him instead of against him. He must project himself as the candidate "of and for the common citizen" … a real statesman. He must project himself as the candidate of truth, justice, and the American way. This 2008 campaign must be a different campaign,

> *Mitt Romney must be a uniter, not a divider.*

not "politics as usual." Mitt Romney must be a "breath of fresh air" in the 2008 campaign.

Foreign Ideas to the Typical Politician. I realize that my ideas are foreign to the typical politician. The name/title politician has earned a very bad reputation (both denotation and connotation). Mitt Romney must not be the typical, run-of-the-mill politician. He must stand head-and-shoulders above all of the other "also-rans."

The Great Hope for the Future. Mitt Romney must project himself as "the great hope for the future." He must be a true conservative. He should hit the Mormon problem (that is what you all seem to be calling it) head on. However, he should turn a negative into a positive by showing what a true, good Mormon is. You must not do this by blood-and-guts politics. You do it through a Ronald Reagan approach to campaigning.

Answers to FAQs. Now, here are my answers to frequently asked questions (FAQs):

1) *Does Mitt Romney really have a religion problem?* No, Mitt Romney does not really have a religion problem. It is just a perception problem (wrong as it is) that people have that we can neutralize by applying Approach #4. Look at this positively. This is a great challenge to possess. Look at how much the media will focus on it providing Mitt Romney

with much more opportunity and exposure to address the American people than will his opponent ... all at no cost!

The way Mitt approaches this challenge will separate him from his opponent and give him a competitive advantage. He can do it. He possesses the wherewithal to create a great image of himself with the help of the liberal press, liberal media, and Mormon haters.

2) ***Is it hopeless?*** Absolutely not! In fact, this supposed problem gives me much hope. It should give Mitt Romney even more hope. Here is a real opportunity for him to define himself as an honest, moral, straightforward family man, great husband, wonderful father, and superb statesman. The other candidates will not have the advantages and possibilities that Mitt possesses from this challenge.

Mitt must look at this positively as something that will catapult him to the top of the polls. He must not look at this issue as something to avoid, deny, or shun. If he does, then it will become his Achilles heel, and defeat will be a self-fulfilling prophecy. He should welcome it in the grand old Reagan style. *Turn a negative into a super positive.* That is what I say.

> ***Turn a negative into a super positive.***

3) ***Can Mitt address it himself?*** No, Mitt should only answer direct questions directly. However, the "fourth estate" should address this challenge. Yes, you can go ahead and have the third party political organization that addresses this issue. However, I tell you, it will not work as well as using the "fourth estate" as I have defined the term.

4) ***How did John F. Kennedy handle it?*** John Kennedy handled it superbly ... exactly the same way that Mitt Romney will handle it. Do not run away from it. Hit it head on. Make Mitt define himself. Do not let his opponent define him. Be passionate. *Win the hearts and minds of the people through the people.* Stay above the fray.

Do not project the John Kerry image ... the "I am holier than thou" image. Do not project the "wild man" image of Al Gore screaming at the top of his lungs. Do not project the wimpy, anti-

> ***Win the hearts and minds of the people through the people***

American image of Jimmy Carter. Do not project the gigolo image of Bill Clinton. Do not project the "I'm not a crook, expletive deleted" image of Richard "Tricky Dickey" Nixon. Do not project the jock "bump your head" image of Gerald Ford. I can go on and on, but you get my drift. He must project a stable, statesman-like image and be full of integrity.

5) **Can the Mormon Church help Mitt address this issue?** Yes, but the Church needs to remain neutral as it always does and not be obviously involved in partisan politics. That does not mean that the Church cannot attempt to improve its own image through a massive PR campaign to educate the masses about the church for the sole purpose of countering the negative polls about the Church and its image. This will be a missionary effort on a grand scale to improve the Church's image to the average American.

This missionary PR campaign should make no mention of Mitt Romney. However, he will receive the good fallout and by-product from it. Mitt will receive positive results simply by association … because he is a good member of the Church. Do not deny it; do not run away from it; but use it as a positive advantage, not a handicap.

6) **Can anyone else help him address it?** Yes, all reasonable approaches will help. However, the help that will catapult Mitt over the top is the "fourth estate," i.e., the grass-roots Americans, the Republican base, and the average American. Remember, former Congressman Ron Packard (a Southern California Mormon) won his election through a write-in candidacy!

Mitt's own father, George Romney (who was my hero at the time), did not have the Church as a yoke around his neck. In fact, George Romney was at the top of the polls until he went to Vietnam and claimed that he was "brainwashed." From that moment on, his campaign went down the tubes. Mitt should be sure never to commit that same or similar type of mistake.

"Brainwashing" has a definite, finite meaning. We know what "brainwashing" means. Untruths and/or misinformation, perhaps, led George Romney astray, but he was definitely not "brainwashed." To claim that he was "brainwashed" was career limiting for him. Hence, his presidential candidacy "went down the drain just by a slip of the brain."

George Romney was a bishop, stake president, president of American Motors, and Governor of Michigan. Later he became Secretary of Housing and Urban Development (HUD) and a regional representative in the Church. He was more involved with running the Church than is son, Mitt Romney, ever was, yet he did not have the anti-Mormon challenge that faces Mitt. *You would think our country has come a long way in the last three to four decades. However, we have regressed when it comes to religious tolerance by SPs, the extreme left, and the extreme right.*

> *You would think our country has come a long way in the last three to four decades. However, we have regressed when it comes to religious tolerance by SPs, the extreme left, and the extreme right.*

7) ***Should Mitt position himself as "a strong candidate who happens to be Mormon" or "a Mormon who happens to be a strong candidate"?*** Yes, Mitt should present himself as a strong candidate who just happens to be a Mormon. He should not present himself as a Mormon who happens to be a strong candidate. Remember, Joseph Smith was a Mormon who happened to be a strong candidate. However, that did not get him anywhere in the presidential race.

8) ***Does Mitt really have a choice in the matter?*** Mitt Romney has numerous choices in the matter. *Remember, it is not the substance, but the style that wins the hearts and minds of the voters.* He must present himself above the fray, as a uniter, as a statesman, and one who listens to the people. Do not be like

> *Remember, it is not the substance, but the style that wins the hearts and minds of the voters.*

George W. Bush who will not listen to his base but will only follow what he believes to be right. Big mistake!

Mitt should listen to his base. That is a whole lot different than to be guided by the polls as was Bill Clinton. Whatever direction the wind blew is the way he went. Listening to the base means listening to a uniform sampling of his strongest grass-roots supporters and moving forward accordingly.

Some foolish men and women conduct polls as guided by their political affiliation or leanings. Listening to the pollsters makes candidates even more foolish. However, listening to key members of the base is like a stake president who listens to his counselors, high councilors, stake council, and bishoprics. Additionally, a bishop listens to his counselors, Priesthood Executive Committee, Ward Council, and quorum and auxiliary presidencies. Those are not polls.

Those comprise listening to good counsel as with counsel of councils. Mitt Romney must listen to counsel from those who will give them their best judgment, ideas, and opinions, not whimsical politically motivated polling of those who possess hidden agendas.

9) **Would anyone really dare play the religion card in a race against Mitt?** Absolutely! *Opponents definitely will play the religious card on Mitt Romney.* Now, Mitt needs to devise an effective way to counteract it in a engaging but neutralizing manner. He can talk calmly about the early Church and the unfortunate way the non-Mormons persecuted, killed, and drove out the Mormons from Missouri along with the Missouri governor's extermination order.

Mitt needs to point out that we should have came a long way from those days and how prejudice and subtle discrimination need to be abolished from today's America. After all, our forefathers formed the United States on the principle of freedom of religion. Talk about how we Mormons believe that everyone has a right to worship their God in any way they please (wherever, however, and whomever).

> *Opponents definitely will play the religious card on Mitt Romney.*

10) **If so, who are the groups or individuals who would be most likely to play that card?** The extremist liberals will definitely play that card. The bigots and anti-Mormons will play that card. The Hollywood Mafia and Hollywood elite will play that card. The ACLU, atheists, SPs, errant press, and nasty politicians will play that card. Some of the bigoted Protestant religions (e.g., those who made "The God Makers," for example) will play that card. You may even find Black extremists playing that card.

11) **How and when would they be most likely to play it?** They will play the religious card like when they dropped the A-bomb in a TV ad a couple of days before the election showing Barry Goldwater as trigger-happy. Goldwater did not have enough time to recover. They will play the religious card like when Teddy Kennedy did on Mitt Romney in their senate race. They will play the religious card like when they did play the various cards in the midterm campaigns with that idiot Ex-Representative Foley from Texas, the fool George Allen of Virginia, and many others in Missouri, Ohio, and Arizona.

Politics has become a filthy, dirty, blood-sport game played by filthy, dirty, bloody people. I despise politics and politicians ... especially political hacks. Mitt Romney can either reject that kind of feeling or perpetuate it even further during the 2008 campaign. Do not let him perpetuate it!

Currently, I respect this man greatly. If he plays politics as usual, I will continue to despise politics and all politicians, and he will fall from grace in my eyes.

> *Politics has become a filthy, dirty, blood-sport game played by filthy, dirty, bloody people.*

We need more politicians like Zell Miller and Joe Lieberman who put the American people first ... before their party and politicians' lust for power and money. *Mitt Romney can be that next best hope for this country, for by that time, our Constitution may "hang by a thread."*

12) **If it is inevitable that the religion card will be played against Mitt, how can we help him inoculate against its effects?** You inoculate against

it by his responding to it as would a statesman (i.e., Ronald Reagan) and letting the "fourth estate" work the problem.

13) **What are the dangers of an inoculation campaign?** There are no dangers as long as we go about it subtly, methodically, and in a proactive manner. However, if we went about it as a blood sport, then the danger is losing the race.

14) *What are the dangers of doing nothing?* According to Murphy's Law, when left alone, problems usually go from-bad-to-worse. Left alone, this problem will go from-bad-to-worse. So, be proactive and do the right things to inoculate against the naysayers.

A Very Simple Solution. My solution to Mitt's challenges is very simple. Remember, he should never go after a fly with a sledgehammer. Use a fly swatter. He cannot push against a string. Pull on the string. He cannot win people over with anger, hatred, and threats. However, he can win them over with warm fuzzies, sugar and spice, and honey instead of vinegar. Furthermore, he should never forget faith, hope, and charity interspersed with random acts of kindness and love.

A Candidacy of Inclusion, Not Exclusion. Remember, if Mitt Romney will save our country when our Constitution "hangs by a thread" during his first term, he must do it with confidence while bringing all parties to the table together. The Lord said, "*Come now, and let us reason together.*" (Isaiah 1:18) When Mitt Romney approaches his candidacy in that manner, he will be extremely successful. Do otherwise, and he will fail miserably. Above all, do not ever let him say, "*Read my lips; no new taxes.*" As said by a not-very-bright man, that would be the kiss of death.

Take Control of the Media War. I tell you. If you do not take control of this campaign, others will define Mitt Romney and control the campaign. Mitt Romney should define himself. *The whacko, left wing, extremist, radical liberals as well as the whacko, right wing, extremist, radical conservatives will attempt to define Mitt in a*

> *The whacko, left wing, extremist, radical liberals as well as the whacko, right wing, extremist, radical conservatives will attempt to define Mitt in a bad light.*

bad light. He must take control of the media war that will surely continue throughout his entire campaign.

Plan for Countering the Last-minute Bomb. Beware! Wait for the last minute bomb that they will drop within one week of the election. Plan for it. Devise alternative solutions that will neutralize, defuse, and dilute these vitriolic insane leftists as well as insane rightists. Keep Mitt steady, humble, self-effacing, and humorous. Remember, Ronald Reagan! Let your third party and the fourth estate battle these leftists and rightists. Keep Mitt Romney above the fray, righteous, and non-combative (as far as verbal vitriol is concerned). Go get 'em!

Sacred Religious Garments. Remember this: the garments have been on the Internet before (many times before). It is nothing new. Let us not blow it up into something bigger than life. The counter to that is this: we calmly need to chastise people who make a sacrilege out of sacred religious practices. Many religions have various garments (including undergarments) that are no different than what we Mormons have. I have an East Indian friend who was a Zoroastrian. He had an undergarment with sacred markings on it. I had since baptized him and now he wears our garments. It is not that big of a deal!

Other Religions and Fraternal Organizations Use Strange Garments. The Catholics have all kinds of strange garments, robes, sashes, headgear, aprons, and so on as well as do some of the Protestant religions. They both have tremendous symbolism related to their garments and other paraphernalia. Different fraternal organizations have various kinds of garments (clothing) that have all kinds of symbolism related to them as well as initiation practices that are strange. I know; I joined a fraternity while in college.

Avoid "Breaking News" Revelations. Hence, the Mormon garments are nothing new. *We have sacred things, not secret things.* We have nothing to be ashamed of and nothing to hide. We just need to bring these things out and discuss them before they throw them to the public in big, phony "Breaking News" revelations. We must vector the momentum and direction of the campaign. Do not let others direct it for us. Charge!

> *We have sacred things, not secret things*

Appendix F

Bob Uda's AT and CT Background

Bob Uda has been somewhat involved in antiterrorism (AT), counterterrorism (CT), and security-related activities in some form or another over the past quarter century of his career. In particular, he is keenly interested in CT and performs focused research in this area.

AT and CT Experience

- Prepared the "Initial Action Plan (IAP) for Homeland Security" while at The Titan Corporation to involve the corporation in anti-and counterterrorism.

- Worked with the former mayor of San Diego, who headed the Titan Office of Homeland Security (TOHS) at the time.

- Conducted extensive research and intelligence gathering on anti-and counterterrorism.

- Prepared a 22-page white paper on "Ideas and Concepts for Combating Terrorism."

Emerging Antiterrorism Technologies

- Worked with the president and CEO of the Titan Emerging Technologies and Businesses Segment and prepared the Strategic Operating Plan (SOP).

- The SOP covered such topics as pulsed corona reactor (PCR) system for destroying biological agents, pathogens, and toxins; biometric security systems; suspect database; and automated identification (ID) system.

Irradiation Technology for Food and Mail

- Prepared the SureBeam Saudi Technologies Joint Venture Business Plan/ Proposal, which won a $50 million contract.

- Used irradiation technologies (predominantly electron beam and X-ray technologies) to cold-pasteurize food products to kill food-borne bacteria including E-coli, Salmonella, Listeria, and Campylobacter.

- Prepared Titan MailSafe presentation/handouts for Titan's chairman, president, and CEO for presentation to the United States Postal Service (USPS) regarding the irradiation of postal mail against anthrax and other biological warfare agents.

Research on Physical Security Threats

- Won a $50K, Phase I Small Business Innovation Research (SBIR) contract from the Air Force Ballistic Missile Office (BMO) and performed research and development (R&D) as Principal Investigator (PI) on the "Definition and Assessment of Physical Security Threats to Small Intercontinental Ballistic Missile (ICBM) Basing Systems."

- Performed this six-month contract and submitted a detailed report on the Phase I project.

- Specific tasks included the following:

  o Performed threat and vulnerability analysis (TVA) on the hard mobile launcher (HML) and fixed hard silo.

  o Characterized the adversary.

  o Developed new, cost-effective countermeasures to mitigate the threats.

  o Prepared and submitted two R&D status reports, a draft final report for BMO review/comments, and incorporated BMO comments into the final report submitted at the end of Phase I.

Physical Security System Studies and Analyses

- Served as Project Manager on a consulting contract with General Dynamics Convair (GDC) on "Peacekeeper Carry Hard Basing (CHB)

Physical Security System Studies and Analyses, Phase I," and prepared a report on this research project.

- Specific tasks included the following:

  o Performed studies, analyses, and support services to assist GDC in defining a physical security system for the Peacekeeper CHB concept point of departure (POD), system definition, and interfacing concealment and security issues.

  o Supported concealment vs. standoff-distance trade studies by providing selection criteria and weighting factors for identified alternative systems.

  o Generated a database and reported the results of an industry/literature search of state-of-the-art electronic sweep and intrusion detection equipment for the defense of the Peacekeeper base and of adversary electronic surveillance equipment that were most effective for the Peacekeeper basing concept.

  o Established acceptance parameters of detection and false alarm rates for the deployment areas.

  o Identified the most effective combination of detection devices for area control.

Physical Security Systems Bibliography

- Prepared "A Bibliography of Physical Security Systems" on a consulting contract with LB&M Associates (now named Advancia Corporation).

- Reviewed classified/unclassified documents relating to physical security systems (PSS).

- Prepared this unclassified report and submitted it to LB&M for their Phase II SBIR contract on "Protecting the Small ICBM" with the USAF BMO.

Plans for Nuclear Security and Safety, System Security, ADP Security, and OPSEC

- Prepared a nuclear security/safety (surety) enhancement program Enhanced System Security Plan (ESSP) for GDC on the Tomahawk Cruise Missile Program.

- Prepared a 24-page input on System Security Engineering, which comprised Chapter 20 of the division-wide GDC System Engineering Manual.

- Prepared the System Security Plan, Automatic Data Processing (ADP) Security Plans, and Operations Security (OPSEC) Plan for General Dynamics Space Systems Division (GD/SSD) on the Medium Launch Vehicle (MLV) Program.

Counterterrorism Conference

- Attended the Asia-Pacific Homeland Security Summit and Expo, sponsored by the State of Hawaii et al, Hilton Hawaiian Village Hotel, Honolulu, Hawaii, 11/14/04-11/17/04, 3 days

Keynote Presentation to ASIS on Physical Security Countermeasures

- Made a keynote presentation on July 1, 1986, to the San Fernando Valley Chapter of the American Society for Industrial Security (ASIS) on "System Security Engineering as It Relates to Physical Security Countermeasures Against Adversaries Such as Terrorists, Guerrillas, and Commandos."

Company Facility Security Officer

- Served as the Facility Security Officer (FSO) for Apollo Systems Technology, Inc. (AST) and prepared the "Standard Practice Procedure (SPP) for Implementing the Requirements of the Industrial Security Manual (ISM) for Safeguarding Classified Information."

Military Service

- Graduated as a distinguished military graduate (DMG) through the four-year Air Force Reserve Officer Training Corps (AFROTC) program at the University of Oklahoma.

- Served on active duty in the USAF as an astronautical development engineer for over eight years on assignments at Air Force Institute of Technology—School of Engineering (AFIT-SE) Wright-Patterson Air Force Base (WPAFB), Dayton, OH; Air Force Satellite Test Center (STC) in Sunnyvale, CA; Headquarters, Space and Missile Systems Organization (SAMSO) (now Space and Missile Systems Center, SMC) in El Segundo, CA; and Air Force Plant Representative Office (AFPRO) at McDonnell Douglas Astronautics Company (MDAC) in Huntington Beach, CA.

- MS in Astronautics from AFIT.

- Graduated from the Air Force Squadron Officer School (SOS).

- Honorably discharged as a Regular Captain in the Air Force.

Past Clearances Held

- Held Top Secret and beyond clearance in the USAF.

- Held Secret clearances at Hamilton Standard Division of United Technology Corporation (UTC), HR Textron Inc., Apollo Systems Technology, Inc., and Rockwell International Space Systems Division.

- Worked in sensitive compartmented information facilities (SCIFs).

- Dealt with WNINTEL (Warning Notice—Intelligence Sources and Methods Involved) information.

Professional Society Memberships

- Member of the International Association for Counterterrorism & Security Professionals (IACSP).

- Member of the International Association of Law Enforcement Intelligence Analysts, Inc. (IALEIA).

- Member of the National Defense Industrial Association (NDIA).

About the Author

Robert T. (Bob) Uda is president, owner, general manager, and principal consultant of Bob Uda and Associates (BU&A). He had served in the United States Air Force for over eight years and in the aerospace and defense industries for a quarter century. He has also worked in the software services, wireless telecommunications, information technology, and electronics industries for seven years. Hence, he has a total of 40 years of professional working experience in the military, aerospace/defense, and other industries.

Bob Uda currently serves as proposal center manager of BAE Systems National Security Solutions (NSS). Bob has served as director of business capture and proposal development of Ocean Systems Engineering Corporation (OSEC); manager of proposal development of L-3 Communications Interstate Electronics Corporation (IEC); director of marketing and proposals at Titan Wireless, Inc.; and manager of business processes, project manager—IT, and senior manager of proposal development at QUALCOMM, Inc.

Furthermore, he served as chairman, president, and CEO of Apollo Systems Technology, Inc.; vice president and general manager at North American Manufacturing Corporation; vice president of business development at Sterling Software, Inc.; and general manager, product line manager, and program manager at HR Textron Inc.

At Rockwell International Space Systems Division, Bob served as project manager, program development manager, manager of advanced programs (proposal development), and member of the technical staff. Furthermore, he served as deputy program manager (project engineer) at TRW Defense and Space Systems Group and astronautical development engineer in the USAF.

Bob earned BS degrees in aerospace engineering from the University of Oklahoma and in general business from Regents College of the University of the State of New York (now named Excelsior College). He further earned an MS degree in astronautics from the Air Force Institute of Technology (AFIT) and an MBA degree from the University of La Verne (California). Furthermore, he received a diploma in The Executive Program in Management from the UCLA Graduate School of Management. Currently, Bob works on an online PhD in

Business Administration (BA) with specialization in Homeland Security (HS) from the Northcentral University (NCU) located in Prescott, Arizona, and plans to graduate in 2010.

Bob has over 40 publications including 12 books. He has served as a full-time professor of systems acquisition management with the Defense Acquisition University (DAU) and taught courses covering program management, systems engineering, and systems acquisition management. As an adjunct faculty lecturer, he taught "Career Development" in the College of Business Administration at the California State University San Marcos. He taught "Writing and Publishing" as an instructor in the Osher Lifelong Learning Institute Program at Cal State San Marcos Office of Extended Studies. Furthermore, he taught logistics graduate students as an adjunct faculty member of National University.

He is a fellow in the British Interplanetary Society, associate fellow in the American Institute of Aeronautics and Astronautics, Certified Manager with the Institute of Certified Professional Managers (ICPM), and a founding charter member of the Association of Proposal Management Professionals. He also serves as an at-large member of the ICPM Board of Regents. Furthermore, he serves as a director and vice president of the International Technology Institute (ITI). Additionally, Bob is a member of the International Association for Counterterrorism & Security Professionals (IACSP), member of the International Association of Law Enforcement Intelligence Analysts, Inc. (IALEIA), and member of the National Defense Industrial Association (NDIA).

Bob Uda was born in Honolulu, Hawaii, and lived in Hawaii for 20 years. He is the third of seven children of Masao and Irene Kuualoha Uda (both deceased).

Internationally recognized in community service, Bob appears in 46 Who's Who publications including Who's Who in the World, Who's Who in America, Who's Who in California, Who's Who in Science and Engineering, and Who's Who in Finance and Industry. You can contact Bob Uda by e-mail at bobuda@ roadrunner.com.

Index

978-0-595-42818-2
0-595-42818-5